Global Practice in World History:
Advances Worldwide

Global Practice in World History
Advances Worldwide

Edited by Patrick Manning

Markus Wiener Publishers
Princeton

Copyright © 2008 by Patrick Manning
All rights reserved. No part of this book may be reproduced or transmitted in any form or by any means, electronic or mechanical, including photocopying, recording, or by any information storage and retrieval system, without permission of the copyright holder.

For information write to:
Markus Wiener Publishers
231 Nassau Street, Princeton, NJ 08540
www.markuswiener.com

Book design by Robin Luo
Cover design by Lisa Jeanne Graf

Library of Congress Cataloging-in-Publication Data
Global Practice in World History : Advances Worldwide / edited by Patrick Manning.
 p. cm.
Includes bibliographical references.
ISBN 978-1-55876-500-9 (alk. paper) Hardcover
1. World history—Study and teaching (Higher)
I. Manning, Patrick, 1941–D16.2.G55 2007
907.1'1--dc22   2007038264
Paperback ISBN 978-1-55876-501-6

Printed in the United States of America on acid-free paper

Contents

Preface
Patrick Manning   vii

Debates and Directions in Research

1. Mapping World History: Report on the
   World History Research Agenda Symposium   1
   David Christian, Marilyn Lake, and Potukuchi Swarnalatha

World and Global History in the University

2. Monographic and Macro Histories: Confronting Paradigms   23
   Diego Olstein

3. World History from an Islamic Perspective: The Experience
   of the International Islamic University Malaysia   39
   Ahmed Ibrahim Abushouk

4. Creating Global History from Asian Perspectives   57
   Shigeru Akita

5. Teaching Modern Global History at Nankai:
   A Noncentric and Holistic Approach   69
   Zhang Weiwei

6. World History and Global Studies at the University of Leipzig   81
   Matthias Middell and Katja Naumann

7. Global History and Economic History: A View of the
   L.S.E. Experience in Research and Graduate Teaching   99
   Gareth Austin

8. Directing Research in World History at
   Washington State University   113
   Heather Streets

Institutions Sustaining World History

  9. The *Journal of World History*   129
     Jerry H. Bentley

 10. The Significance of the Research Institute for World History
     (NPO-IF) in Japan   141
     Shingo Minamizuka

 11. Museums and World History   155
     Leslie Witz

 12. The World History Network, Inc.—Facilitating
     Global Historical Research   167
     Patrick Manning

Notes on Contributors   179

Preface

The contents of this volume confirm that sophisticated study of world history is progressing in many regions of the planet and in various institutional settings. One should not be surprised to hear discussion of world affairs and world history in every corner—contemporary interactions have put phrases about globalization on every tongue. What is exciting, and what is likely to broaden and deepen the understanding of our shared past, is the emergence of formal institutions for study of world history. University departments, research institutes, international conferences, and the leaders of museums are now demonstrably involved in full-scale study of the human past at a global level. The results will surely reveal new patterns, dispel some old beliefs, provoke debates, and demonstrate the need for still more research.

This is the second volume in a series on research in world history produced by the World History Network, Inc. The previous volume, *World History: Global and Local Interactions* (2005), displayed the accomplishments of PhD students and graduates whose research focused on topics in world history. In that volume, twelve specialists in world history published results of PhD dissertations completed in the U.S. (and one in Europe). Their studies, characterized by breadth and precision, traced the links of global and local influences in various areas of human experience. In sum, they confirmed that world historical research at the PhD level can lead to valid results, and that it has prepared these scholars for full careers of analyzing global historical questions.

This second volume, in turn, focuses on the practice and institutional setting of world-historical research. It displays research and teaching in world history as it is practiced in universities and other institutions around the world. The fifteen contributors work at fourteen institutions in ten countries dispersed across five continents. Each of the institutions described represents a remarkable achievement, brought into service through insight and determination of the authors and their colleagues..

The plan for the book took practical shape in June and July of 2005. Virtually all of the authors were present at either the World History Association meeting at Al-Akhwayn University in Morocco (June 2005) or the International Congress of Historical Sciences meeting in Sydney

(July 2005), where world and global historians were convened at a meeting hosted by Marnie Hughes-Warrington and Adrian Carton of Macquarie University. At these two meetings, the growing interest of world and global historians in collaborating across national and regional boundaries became evident, and most of the authors accepted invitations to prepare chapters for this volume. Three further international meetings provided opportunities for exchange among the authors: the European Network in Universal and Global History (ENIUGH) conference of October 2005 in Leipzig, the World History Association (WHA) annual meeting of June 2006 in Long Beach, and the World History Research Agenda Symposium of November 2006 in Boston.

The most general of the chapters is placed first: it is the official report of the Research Agenda Symposium. In this opening chapter, David Christian, Marilyn Lake, and Potukuchi Swarnalatha provide a synthesis and commentary on this unusual conference, which launched the formal discussion of priorities in world-historical research. Fifty historians convened in Boston to compare, contrast, and rank the various approaches and topics in world history. The results showed how many choices in research have yet to be made, yet confirm that world historians are preparing to work collaboratively to allocate their limited resources as wisely as possible. This 2006 meeting was important for itself and also because it sets the framework for a second such meeting, scheduled for 2009.

The seven chapters of the second section describe university-level study of world history at undergraduate and especially graduate levels. Authors working on three continents convey some remarkable advances in conceptualization of the global past, in time frames ranging from millennia to decades. Equally important, the authors explain the curricula they have implemented and the techniques they use for directing advanced students in world historical research. The third section of the book turns from university departments of history to the other institutions that support research in world history: journals, museums, and research institutes. Here the authors document the organizational innovations that have brought discussion of world-historical issues to wider audiences.

Overall, these chapters present the thinking and the activities of some of the most serious and successful practitioners of world history. They confirm the existence of an emerging world-wide discourse on the past of our planet, but they also reveal the distinctive conditions and local innovations of global historians in different parts of the world. While the study of world history remains uneven, so that some of the most privileged regions have been able to devote more resources to its study, the pages of this volume tend to suggest that no part of the world is lacking in scholars and readers who are considering seriously the large-scale patterns of the human past and present.

For assistance in the preparation of this volume, I wish to thank the School of Arts & Sciences at the University of Pittsburgh for financial support, Robin Luo for the design of the book, and Markus Wiener for his generosity and insight as publisher.

Patrick Manning
Pittsburgh, June 2007

CHAPTER I

Mapping World History:
Report on the World History Research Agenda Symposium

David Christian, Marilyn Lake, and Potukuchi Swarnalatha

The "Research Agenda Symposium—Research in World History: Connections and Globalizations" conference met in Boston at the John Hancock Conference Center, on November 10–12, 2006. It was organized by a committee chaired by Pat Manning of the University of Pittsburgh. Sponsors included the University of Pittsburgh, the World History Network, and the World History Association.[1] This summary of some of the issues raised and discussed during the conference is intended, first, as a record for participants of some of the research agendas and strategies debated during the conference. It is also intended to help other historians, as well as funding agencies, to get some sense of the range of research problems being tackled by world historians.[2]

Each of the thirty-six participants at the Symposium delivered a five-minute proposal on research agendas for world history; all proposals had been circulated in advance and posted on the conference website. Of the participants, eighteen came from institutions in the United States and eighteen from outside the U.S., making this one of the most internationally representative of recent conferences on world history held under the auspices of the World History Association. In addition to the formal participants, there were ten observers and six members of the conference committee. The conference program is included as an appendix to this chapter.

The initial call for papers invited research proposals on "the full range of world-historical issues," including "any issues and approaches that may elucidate our understanding of world history." In the introductory session, Adam McKeown asked if it was possible to construct "a consensus statement on the research project of world history," and to find "modes of cooperation" among researchers in world history.[3] The call for papers included the following tentative list of possible areas of discussion:[4]

- Topics that should be high priorities in world-historical research
- Debates requiring further research
- Time frame
- Disciplines and disciplinary connections requiring particular attention
- Methods of world-historical research requiring emphasis
- Resources—archives and other documentation—requiring attention
- Analytical emphasis—for instance, global patterns or global-local connections
- Individual or collaborative work
- Organization of national or transnational research groups
- Relative emphasis on graduate study, work by senior faculty, or combinations

What follows is an attempt to summarize and comment on the intense and diverse discussions that took place over the one-and-a-half days of the conference. It is inevitably selective, and cannot do justice to the immense variety of ideas and perspectives that were presented, or to the intellectual synergy that the conference generated. Though we have attempted a coherent account of these debates, we have tried to avoid tidying up all the loose ends, as an excessively neat account could not possibly convey the diverse, rich, and often unresolved nature of the discussions. As the reader will see, the conference raised as many questions as answers about world history and its future. The summary is in three sections, followed by a conclusion:

1. A summary of the main research areas and strategies discussed in the formal presentations and discussions;
2. An attempt to summarize the diverse but overlapping definitions of world history proposed or implied in the course of these discussions;

3. Commentary and discussion of possible priorities in world history research and future directions for the discipline.

Research Areas and Strategies

The proposals (available on the conference website) can be classified in several different ways. The classifications themselves provide insight into how world historians currently organize their research. But the classificatory straitjacket adopted here cannot possibly capture the fluidity of discussions which ranged widely in space, time and theme.

Spatial scales. Most world historians are keen to escape the national frames that have shaped so much historical scholarship. But what alternatives are available? Several presentations defined their themes around broad geographical regions and the relationship of those regions to world history in recent centuries. Regions mentioned included China, the Middle East, the Indian sub-continent, the Pacific Rim, and the Caribbean. In all cases, it was understood that world historians will naturally attempt to see these regions in larger spatial and temporal contexts, and to understand both the temporal coherence of each region, and the complex ways in which it is embedded within global networks and processes. The regional perspective is vital to world history because global issues are always seen from particular regional perspectives.[5] . One may attempt at once to "globalize the local" and "localize the global." Such attempts can help world history and its constituent strategies to achieve multicultural understanding—an understanding of the nuances of transnationalism as embedded aspects of world history.[6]

Chronological scales. Many papers defined their themes chronologically or by particular eras. By doing so, they raised a large methodological question: how has the issue of chronological scale and the idea of linearity shaped world-historical scholarship. A striking feature of the conference was the overwhelming concentration of research in world history on recent centuries and the modern era.[7] As Boris Stremlin put it: "the kind of world history that most people here subscribe to, the kind of world history that's promoted by the World History Association, is essentially the pre-history of globalization."[7] Pat Manning commented: "Within the community of world historians, of course there is a great deal of concentration on modern times, but that merely mirrors the historical profession as a whole."[8]

The minority of papers focusing on larger time scales discussed the need to study pre-modern definitions of and approaches to world history, to describe the human relationship with the biosphere in large temporal frameworks, to explore particular themes (such as art or religion or the evolution of cosmologies) over millennia, and to explore the possibilities for a coherent world history of humanity as a whole.[10] It was argued that the large-scale view has acquired increased urgency in an era in which significant challenges (including the threats of nuclear war, world poverty, and global warming) can only be tackled by a unified global community.[11]

Several papers touched on the importance of exploring particular themes on larger chronological scales. The themes mentioned in this context included peace and violence, art, state formation, maritime history, and religion.[12] Discussions of distinct eras also raised issues of regional continuities and connections, which were related, in turn, to the larger issue of periodization. Can there be global periodizations that escape the tyranny of the Western model? Or is periodization by its very nature local or regional?

Historiography, conceptual and methodological issues. Several papers posed historiographical questions about the nature of world history, its evolution, its regional differences, and its role in the modern world. One group of papers touched on differing perspectives on world history in different parts of the world, and the need to broaden our sense of what world history is, has been, and can be.[13] In a comment, Peter Gran asked whether world historians should aim at a unified vision of world history (in the spirit of some forms of Marxism), or a diverse vision (in a spirit of liberalism). He suggested that the very structure of this conference implied a broad commitment to a pluralist vision.[14]

Most papers in this group touched on the question of whether world history as practiced, particularly in North America, reflects a "Western" rather than a global perspective on the past.[15] Does that perspective reflect the historical agency or political power of the West? If so, is there a danger that historians based in the West may (unwittingly?) impose a distinctly Western vision of world history?[16] How might they respond to the call for Europe to be "provincialized"?[17] If world historians are to be truly global in their approach it is surely vital that they widen their view of what world history can be, by adopting a more "cosmopolitan" approach, incorporating perspectives from diverse regions and eras, and also from writers who are not professional historians.[18] A related group of papers touched on conceptual aspects of world history, in particular the notion of networks and nodes as an alternative to the dominant idea of the nation.[19]

Several papers suggested that world historians could engage more forthrightly in public debate on global issues, assuming a more active role as public intellectuals with a distinctive perspective on today's world.[20] To be sure, many historians already write for newspapers and magazines and engage with the electronic media, but one participant suggested that aspiring world historians might benefit from special training, as part of postgraduate training, in skills such as the writing of op-ed pieces.[21]

A related issue concerns the nature of the audience for world history. Who are our readers and what do they need or expect from world historians?[22] Is there a global audience, or are there many distinctive regional and local audiences for world history, each with its own interests and expectations? Traditionally, the writing of history has been intertwined with the making of identities, whether national, ethnic, sexual, or racial. History has played a major role in shaping national identifications and constructing national audiences in turn. Will the practice of world history construct global audiences who increasingly imagine themselves as global citizens?

Methodological discussions touched on the question of whether world historians should begin with the details or the overview. Do we need more information and more databases? Or, instead, is the main need for clearer synoptic frameworks and a more carefully constructed conceptual toolkit?[23] This discussion touched on a larger issue that simmered below the surface for most of the conference: should world historians aim at a synoptic and global view of history, or should they avoid constructing more grand narratives and focus, rather, on interconnections and comparisons, on the multiple strands from which world history is constructed?

The issue of "interdisciplinarity" surfaced in many discussions. Is world history intrinsically interdisciplinary? If so, *how* interdisciplinary? Will world history necessarily encourage collaboration with scholars in the natural sciences as well as in other disciplines in the humanities or social sciences? Should it try to build on the models and paradigms available in other historically oriented disciplines, from sociology to cosmology? Should world historians engage in intellectual "outreach," seeking new forms of collaboration within and beyond the history discipline? Should we accept that historical studies now extend to a range of historical disciplines including biology, geology, and cosmology? (If so, should these disciplines be sharing conferences and constructing collaborative research teams?)

Themes. Many papers centered on particular themes. Major themes included religion,[24] art,[25] violence,[26] peace,[27] cities,[28] ecology,[29] disease,[30] maritime history,[31] state formation,[32] international exchanges of ideas,[33] technology and communications,[34] and a mix of development, economic history and "defensive modernization."[35] Some historical topics are clearly natural candidates for world-historical scholarship, a case that Ingo Heidbrink made eloquently for the study of maritime history, Hans-Heinrich Nolte for the study of violence, and Roland Wenzlhuemer for the study of communications technologies.[36] So it is perhaps no surprise that the largest group of thematic papers focused on another intrinsically international theme, that of migration and regional connections.[37]

Absences in world-historical scholarship. Several commentators noted themes and approaches of importance that were missing or touched on surprisingly little. Two such themes stood out: gender and environmental history. Has world history been a "masculinist," as well as a "Western" project? Has it simply magnified the traditional conceptual divide between the "public" and the "private," the "political" and the "personal," and thus marginalized work on the history of gender and sexuality? Whether one's research focus be cities, religion, migration, or violence, it is clear that gender as a category of analysis ought to be crucial to conceptualizing the human past.

The question was also raised as to whether world history had in fact been too human-centered, and insufficiently conscious of humanity's relations with, and dependence on, the biosphere.[40] Robin and Steffen, in their conference statement, suggested we may be at the beginning of a new geological era, the "Anthropocene," in which humans themselves have become major agents of biospheric change.[41] Both the history of gender and the history of human relations with the environment are clearly important themes for world historians. Thinking about their relative absence from the conference raises conceptual issues about how world history has been understood.

Collaboration and funding. Several papers and comments discussed the potential importance of collaborative scholarship, and the need to consider creating international networks of linked researchers.[42] Many papers on particular themes also stressed the need for broad collaboration. Indeed, it was suggested that collaborative scholarship may be particularly strategic for world history because of the scale of our projects and diversity of skills the field requires.⁴³ So the idea of webs or networks turns out to be important for world history both as a concept (a description of what many world historians study) and as a research strategy. In many fields, including environmental history and the histories of cities and technology, for example, collaboration will have to extend beyond the humanities disciplines to colleagues in the sciences. A related issue concerns funding. Will networks of world historians, perhaps working with colleagues in other disciplines and countries, find it easier to generate research funding than those working solo?

What shapes the balance of themes and approaches? World historians are clearly distinctive in their willingness to explore an unusually wide range of spatial and temporal scales, and to do so, if necessary, by crossing discipline boundaries. Yet the themes and approaches apparent at this conference also suggest that the agendas of world history have been shaped to a considerable extent by the preoccupations of historians in general. For example, most of the papers presented were concerned with recent centuries, and most tackled themes that are central to modern historical scholarship. The "world" aspect of world history was apparent less in specific choices of themes and questions than in the approaches to those questions, so it seems that the thematic agendas of world history are largely set by the history profession in general and it is probably unrealistic to expect the field of world history to generate quite separate themes and research agendas. On the other hand, the concern with issues of global interpretation and scale is surely a defining feature of world history.

Professional training in world history. The fact that the themes and approaches of world historians are shaped by the agendas of the larger history profession reflects the background and training of most world historians. There are very few senior historians for whom the idea of world history was so central during their graduate training that they define themselves professionally first and foremost as world historians. On the other hand, many of the emerging cohort of "professional world historians" were present at this meeting, including Eric Martin, David Kalivas, Tiffany Trimmer, George Dehner, Deborah Johnston, and Parker James. The shortage of world history specialists persists largely because there are few programs that train world historians as world historians; nor is there any agreement as to what might be expected of those appointed to jobs in world history.[44]

The issue of professional training in dedicated world history graduate programs is linked to that of funding since, without a clear sense of what it is that distinguishes a professional world historian from other types of historians, it is harder to get the attention of funding agencies. It seems likely that increasing professionalization of world history might also shift the agendas of the field by giving it a more distinctive and disciplinary identity, emphasizing in particular issues of spatial, geographical, and temporal scale. As this conference demonstrated, even world historians find it difficult to take seriously the "global" time frame of 200,000 years, or to incorporate serious discussion of the Paleolithic era into accounts of world history. How would a more serious consideration of very large scales affect discussions of continuities and discontinuities over the long span of human history? Such perspectives might also raise in more acute forms questions about the community whose history world historians are attempting to construct, and about new ways of balancing accounts of the intimate and private with accounts of large patterns and global forces.[45]

Teaching world history. Many discussions touched on the important relationship between teaching and scholarship in world history. To what extent have the agendas of world-historical scholarship been driven by classroom syllabi in world history, and to what extent has the best scholarship in world history shaped teaching texts in the field? Such questions were not the central focus of this conference, which was concerned primarily with world-historical scholarship and research, but there is clearly room for systematic exploration of the distinctive relationship between teaching and scholarship in world history. Some conference statements touched on syllabi and curriculum frameworks with an emphasis on critical thinking and analytical skills.[46] History textbooks, though confined to undergraduate and secondary teaching levels, seem to have made substantial progress in approaching history with a focus on the large issues that determine the contours of the changing world and its societies.

Definitions: What is World History?

This section of our overview addresses more explicitly the issues raised by conference participants with regard to definitions of world history, its purpose and place. What are the spatial and chronological contours of world history? Is world history the same as global history or transnational history or universal history, categories that are sometimes used interchangeably? In a recent "Conversation" on transnational history in *American Historical Review*, Sven Beckert made the point that global, transnational and world history have "much in common" as new "ways of seeing." "They are all engaged in a project to reconstruct aspects of the human past that transcend any one nation-state, empire, or other politically defined territory."[47] But there are important differences among these interpretive projects, especially in goals, methods, and scope, as indicated by the advocates of the various alternatives.[48] For transnational history, the concepts of circulation and flows—of ideas, goods, people, germs, texts—are usually central to the historical analysis.[49] World history usually engages—in addition or instead—with ideas of global themes and stories about the human past with a view to providing new understandings of the history of the world. There can be no prescriptions, however. One's research questions will determine the appropriate frame of analysis and one's conceptualization of each project.

Diversity and coherence in world history. As already indicated, the themes, approaches, and methods described in the papers and discussions were extremely diverse. Clearly, the label, "world history," embraces great thematic and methodological variety, different regional and national approaches, differences in scale, themes, approach, and questions. Multiple approaches to "world history" also reflect a variety of standpoints outside the academy. As Leslie Witz pointed out, the study of such a topic as world heritage sites—what counts as a world heritage site and why—provides a powerful way of teasing out assumptions about world history that are current outside the academic historical discipline.[50]

World history means different things in different cultural contexts. There is a strong U.S. tradition of world history but one of the central challenges of world history as a project will be to negotiate the differences in approach and themes that distinguish different national or regional traditions of world history scholarship. Clearly, regional traditions of world history scholarship are shaped by global power relations as well as local historiographical traditions. World history will need to become more cosmopolitan to accommodate the idea of dispersed historical agency and historical sites. What will it mean to produce a genuinely global tradition of world history scholarship? This question is closely linked to the question of audiences. Can there be a global audience for world history scholarship, or will the needs of different audiences (divided by class or cultural traditions or religious traditions) require different forms of world history? In other words, is world history bound to fragment into various interpretive projects and distinctive regional traditions?

Beneath the diversity of world history there lies, nevertheless, a coherence that is most apparent in approach and perspective. During the discussions, the question was raised: What is the "value added" to the idea of history by the adjectival noun "world?"[51] At the most general level, the phrase "world history" expresses a willingness to move beyond existing national, regional and chronological frameworks, to experiment with a variety of different conceptual, spatial and temporal scales that raise new types of questions and encourage new forms of comparative and interactive study.[52] But it is clear, too, that world history must find ways of linking the different scales, which is why the theme of connections between the global and the local was so prominent, with many participants insisting that these be seen not as discrete separate domains, but mutually constitutive and ever changing.[53]

How should world historians handle specific historical themes while retaining a sense of the coherence of their discipline? World historians seek out themes such as migration or disease or the history of violence, whose development is likely to take historical research beyond conventional national or regional frameworks. They explore issues such as state formation or the impact of religious thought across large periods of time. Many practitioners are attracted to the challenge of identifying larger patterns in human history as a whole, perhaps even providing alternative grand narratives. What distinguishes research and teaching in world history is the willingness to explore beyond and between the scales and themes of most other areas of historiography—a research strategy that can generate new questions and insights. As yet, though, this exploration is still being approached with conceptual and even chronological tools familiar within most other areas of historical scholarship. For example, traditional strategies of periodization may offer little to those world historians keen to approach world history as a global narrative.

There is clearly a tension or dialectic within the field of world history between those keen to focus on the construction of larger, over-reaching narratives at multiple spatial and chronological scales (who see world history as a sort of "connective tissue," in the words of Peter Adebayo) or a potential "pan-human narrative" (as described by Kimball); and those preferring to see world history as opening new possibilities for a multiplicity of approaches to the past, without aiming at the construction of any kind of total narrative. The sense of this meeting was that this should be regarded as a creative tension, rather than a barrier to progress.

Importance and contemporary relevance. Why does world history matter? If it is true that world history, like all forms of history, studies the past in order to illuminate the present, what is the distinctive illumination that world history can provide? One answer, occasionally expressed explicitly, but more often just beneath the surface of discussions and presentations, was that a global or transnational perspective is particularly salient in a global and transnational world. If a world of nation states demanded knowledge of the history of one's own society, perhaps a more globalized world demands the historical perspectives of world history. Is the development of world history a reflection of the increasing number of problems (such as nuclear proliferation, world poverty, or global warming) that can no longer be tackled at national scales? If the growth of world history is driven in part by processes of "globalization," then it might be expected that the discipline has important insights into such processes. If so, does this mean that world historians should attempt a larger vision of human history by borrowing concepts and paradigms from the natural sciences and attempting to construct a narrative of humanity as a whole? Is it possible that humanity as a whole can be thought of as an "imagined" community, analogous conceptually to the national "imagined communities" famously defined by Benedict Anderson a couple of decades ago? Nevertheless, as William Clarence-Smith pointed out, the idea of humanity as a historical community is at least as old as the oldest "universal" religions.[54] Questions about the audience for world history make it easier to pose such questions in practical, as well as theoretical terms. But it is also clear that attention to issues of contemporary relevance raises the question of whether present-centeredness in world history scholarship distorts our understanding of the past.

A related issue concerns the importance of world history within historical scholarship in general. How can, or should, world history, with its distinctive concern for questions and themes at larger scales, help shape developments in other branches of historiography? One answer is that world history, like women's history or economic history or art history, is well placed to encourage closer relations with neighboring disciplines and with scholars around the world. Women's history is instructive in this regard, with its emphasis on interconnections, both as methodology and the subject of research, but also as exemplifying the global connections that can be forged between researchers through conferences, symposia, journals, and collective research projects.

A third issue of contemporary relevance is the relationship between scholarship and teaching. As a teaching discipline, the importance of world history clearly lies in its transnational vision of the human past. But how should that vision be realized? Should it be multiple, diverse, cosmopolitan, or national? Are distinctive regional traditions of world-historical teaching inevitable in a world where many teachers of world history are paid by national governments? Or, to return to a question touched on before, should world historians construct teachable accounts of world history that try to transcend regional and cultural boundaries and prejudices? It has already been suggested that there is a significant divide within world history scholarship between those who seek a unifying vision of the past—new grand narratives—and those who would encourage a multiplicity of visions of the past. This divide also appears also in discussions about world history as a teaching discipline.

Prioritizing Research Agendas and Selecting Future Directions

Though the issue was largely avoided during the conference itself, those of us summarizing the discussions have been invited to comment on the issues raised, as well as to summarize, the discussions. One crucial issue is that of priority. Is there any way of ranking research agendas? Is there any way of teasing from these discussions a world history equivalent of the Hilbert program in mathematics?[55] Conference participants shied away from any attempt to rank research proposals, which suggests that, even if the field is united by a determination to explore multiple scales and themes that cut across regions and disciplines, there is, as yet, little agreement on central themes and research agendas. There does exist within world history a "gravitational pull" towards themes and questions that are posed at larger-than-usual spatial or temporal scales or towards themes and questions that transcend national or regional borders. And in recent years, many world historians have worked hard to move beyond traditional Eurocentric agendas, creating a flourishing scholarship as they do so.[56] However, once we move beyond these unifying assumptions and approaches, there seems to be less unity among world historians about what they ought to be researching.

So can we begin to prioritize by picking out "certain issues or approaches for particular attention" or those topics that "were well presented and show particular promise"?[57] It may help to begin by trying to isolate those features of the papers that were "worldly" or global in implication as opposed to those that might have been presented at any number of other historical conferences. What follows is a tentative list in random order of broad research themes and approaches that emerged either directly or indirectly at the conference. While the first two paragraphs suggest strategic areas of future scholarship, the rest are more concerned with research strategies that may prove particularly salient for the future of world history as a research field.

Historiography and world history. Several papers touched on historiographical issues: on differences in regional approaches to the field, the difficulty of constructing an appropriate conceptual apparatus for world history, or a viable global periodization. Clearly, there is room for a major collaborative project that describes and takes stock of different approaches to world history. These approaches include large-scale interpretations written in recent and earlier times, and also assessments of the role of various regions in world history.[58] Such studies should survey not just scholarly research in world history, but also works produced outside the academy, textbooks for colleges and high schools (the way most people learn about world history),[59] as well as debates on world history in other fora, such as debates over world heritage sites. In the final session, Marnie Hughes-Warrington announced the intention of several participants to form an "International Historiography Research Cluster."[60] Its aims would be: 1. to foster understanding of the institutions, forms and purposes of world histories and historiographies in various socioeconomic and historical contexts; 2. to better understand world history in relationship to history and other forms of historiography; 3. to elaborate the historiography of world history in order to reflect on the different scales and spatial frameworks of the field; and 4. to identify opportunities to undertake collaborative research projects, disseminate results, and engage in the collaborative training of research students.

Exploring multiple time frames. Papers at this conference revealed clearly how many current studies remain centered on recent times. Whereas transnational history clearly has reference to the emergence of nation-states, a defining feature of world history is its historical reach—its frame is the whole of the human past. If the project is to take more seriously the commitment to multiple time scales, its practitioners will find it fruitful to explore the many novel insights and comparative themes available for study on larger scales. At the center of these explorations may be the interdisciplinary challenge of incorporating a broad understanding of the Paleolithic world into discussions of themes including religion, peace and violence, power structures, gender relations, and migration.

Databases and resource collections. There is a need for databases that bring together data over large periods and large areas and are tailored to the distinctive needs of world historians. Such resources, where they can be assembled, will be a crucial part of the comparative and connecting mission of world-historical research. Web-based resources including bibliographies and databases may prove particularly important because they can be widely accessible and can be easily searched. Precise economic data can be assembled for recent centuries and, though with much less precision, for many millennia. There is also room to assemble databases, based on approximations and reasonable interpolations, for the whole span of human history. Such databases might include estimates of population growth, both globally and in different regions, or discussions of the scale and reach of state power, or the nature of violence, or the scale and geography of global patterns of migration. In fact, research on most of the large themes discussed in this conference could be enhanced by the compilation of systematic databases with a broad geographical and chronological reach. (A promising model is the China Historical GIS program at Harvard, under Peter Bol, which is collaborative, high-tech, and correlates many sorts of data to provide a really enhanced historical record over two millennia.)[61] There is also a clear need for a bibliography of resources in world history and related fields that reflects the thematic, chronological, and geographical breadth of the field.[62]

Organizational challenges. Organizational challenges for world history include the construction of an international network of world history associations and support for regional or local networks of world history scholars and teachers, so as to increase the amount of global dialogue and collaboration on world history. Pat Manning reported that plans are underway for the construction of an "International Network of World History Organizations" that will apply for membership of the International Congress of Historical Sciences in time to take part in the 2010 conference of ICHS in Amsterdam.[63]

Graduate programs and the issue of professionalization. A related issue is the importance of encouraging and supporting graduate programs in world history and expanding the number of upper-level courses that can help world history expand and develop its role as a research discipline. Many, particularly those actively engaged in graduate training in world history, feel that this is a vital step towards expanding the number of practicing world historians, and increasing the visibility of world history as a branch of historical scholarship.[64] Increasing professionalization should also make it easier to generate research funding. But it is equally important for historians trained specifically in world history to be able to feel a sense of professional community, develop a distinctive scholarly agenda, and engage in related epistemological and historiographical discussion. Some speakers noted the difficulties graduate students were bound to face in tackling the world historical themes in research theses and expressed some skepticism about pursuing Ph.D dissertations in the field.[65] Others, however, pointed out that sharply focused themes can often make for fine world history scholarship and that there are already several excellent doctoral problems in world history across a range of countries.

Interdisciplinary collaboration. To the extent that world history is defined by its interest in adopting a wide-angle perspective, it should naturally encourage increasing cooperation between historians and scholars in neighboring disciplines. Cooperation with geographers using GIS technology was one area mentioned at the conference.[66] But there are many obvious areas where world historians are strategically placed to encourage greater interdisciplinary activity, even with scholars in the sciences.[67] Such activity should make it easier to develop a historiography that treats human societies as a part of an evolving biosphere rather than as an entirely self-contained domain of scholarship.

Conclusion

The Research Agenda Symposium on World History provided a rare opportunity for scholars in a rapidly developing field to take stock and share ideas about where the field is going. The discussions were wide-ranging and engaged and they displayed the intellectual enthusiasm that characterizes the field as a whole. World history has ancient roots. But as a field of *scientific* scholarship, it is new, which is why enthusiasm is balanced by considerable uncertainty and even anxiety about the field's current status and future directions.[68] In recent decades, world history has generated a rich body of scholarship.[69] This conference showed that there is an astonishing diversity in the approaches, themes, and methods in the field. The conference raised questions about the coherence of world history scholarship, while also illustrating the field's vibrancy, openness, and pluralism. What emerged from these discussions was less a coherent set of research proposals than the teasing out of important areas of debate within the field. Adam McKeown, one of the conference organizers, pointed out in a subsequent comment that the very nature of these debates may help define the field. They included: "The need for graduate training; the appropriateness of the global v. local dichotomy; the value of engaging with world historians from other times and places; the extent to which we need to engage in the metatheory of rethinking our spatial and temporal assumptions (or, more modestly, what can and can't we know at different spatial and temporal scales?); the extent to which world history should look for commonalities or differences." We suspect most participants left the conference with a similar sense of the powerful intellectual synergies such debates can generate within the field of world history and a greater sense of the field's possibilities.

Since the conference concluded, the World History Network and the World History Association have decided to continue this debate by organizing a second conference on research agendas in world history in the 2008-2009 academic year.

APPENDIX: The Program and Participants.

Program: Research Agenda Symposium
Boston, John Hancock Conference Center
November 10-12, 2006

Note: Participants are listed by affiliation and by country of residence. Panelists marked with an asterisk (*) submitted conference statements but were unable to attend.

Friday, November 10
6:00 PM – 7:00 PM: Reception

Saturday, November 11
9:00 AM – 10:30 AM: Session 1 — Tasks for world historians.
    Moderator: Adam McKeown, Columbia University
    Marnie Hughes-Warrington, Macquarie University (Australia)
        "World History Research: Priorities for an Expanded Vision of the Field."
    David Christian, San Diego State University (U.S.)
        "Strange Parallels in World History."
    *Libby Robin and Will Steffen, Australian National University (Australia)
        "World history without historians?"
    Silvia Pappe, Universidad Autonoma Metropolitana (Mexico)
        "Point Zero – What happened to the so-called universal points of view?"
    Peter Gran, Temple University (U.S.)
        "Priorities for Research and Graduate Education:
        World Historians as Public Intellectuals."
    Boris Stremlin, Binghamton University (U.S.)
        "The Production of World History Outside the West."
    Katja Naumann and Matthias Middell, Leipzig University (Germany)
        "Regimes of Territoriality and Historicization of World History Writing."
    Debin Ma, London School of Economics (U.K.)
        "Understanding Global Economics: Approaches and Agenda."

11:00 AM – 12:30 AM: Session 2 — Social science analysis.
    Moderator: Zvi Ben-dor Benite, New York University (U.S.)
    George Dehner, Wichita State University (U.S.)
        "Research in World History: The Case for Diseases in History."
    Ingo Heidbrink, Deutsches Schiffahrtsmuseum (Germany)
        "Priorities in world-historical research – maritime history aspects."
    Hans-Heinrich Nolte, University of Hannover (Germany)
        "Violence: Comparisons and Interactions."

*John Richards**, Duke University (U.S.)
"*State Formation in World History.*"
Cyrus Veeser, Bentley College (U.S.)
"*Defensive Modernization.*"
Roland Wenzlhuemer, Humboldt University (Germany)
"*The De-Materialisation of Telecommunication as a Research Field for World Historians.*"

2:00 PM – 3:30 PM: Session 3 — Cultural and social analysis.
Moderator: H. Parker James, World History Network, Inc.
Ralph Croizier, University of British Columbia (Canada)
"*Visuality in World History: Some Questions and Some Suggestions.*"
Kathleen Kimball, Water Dragon, Inc. (U.S.)
"*World Art as a World History Research Priority.*"
Leslie Witz, University of the Western Cape (South Africa)
"*World heritage and the challenges to world history.*"
Anne Chao, Rice University (U.S.)
"*The Case for an Intellectual Study of World History.*"
Roger Beck, Eastern Illinois University (U.S.)
"*Religions and Religious Missions in World History: Connectors, dividers, and Globalizers.*"
David Lindenfeld, Louisiana State University (U.S.)
"*Beyond Conversion and Syncretism: Strategies and Processes in Local Encounters with World Religions.*"

4:00 PM – 5:30 PM: Session 4 — Region and place in world history.
Moderator: David Kalivas, Middlesex Community College
***Jerome Teelucksingh**, University of the West Indies (Trinidad and Tobago)
"*Marginalized in the Global Village: The Contribution of the Caribbean to World Civilization, 1492-2006.*"
Zhang Weiwei, Nankai University (China)
"*China's Function in Global History in Perspective.*"
Ali Çaksu, independent scholar (Turkey)
"*Islamic history in world history: Waqf institutions.*"
Potukuchi Swarnalatha, Dhirubhai Ambani International School (India)
"*Enveloping Eurasia into World History: A Framework for Research.*"
John Wills, University of Southern California (U.S.)
"*Why Is China So Big? Comparative Political History and the Continued Relevance of Narrative.*"
Juhani Koponen, University of Helsinki (Finland)
"*When Did Development Start? History of development and developmentalism.*"

Sunday, November 12
8:30 AM – 10:00 AM: Session 5 — Human movement
   Moderator: Deborah Smith Johnston, Lexington High School
   Adapa Satyanarayana, Osmania University (India)
      "Research Agenda for World History: Globalization and Migration Studies."
   Marilyn Lake, LaTrobe University (Australia)
      "Modern Mobilities and Transnational Solidarities."
   Anne Gerritsen, Warwick University (U.K.)
      "Local and Global in the Early Modern World: Local Responses to Global Connections, 1500-1800."
   Peter Adebayo, University of Ilorin (Nigeria)
      "Diaspora, Return Migration and Transnational Networking."
   David Perry, University of Minnesota (U.S.)
      "Trans-regional Exchange and the Transformation of Cities."
   Howard Spodek, Temple University (U.S.)
      "Urbanization: A Key Theme in World History."

10:30 AM – 12:00 AM: Session 6 — Networks and organization of research
   Moderator: Stephen Rapp, Georgia State University
   Annette Skovsted Hansen, Aarhus University (Denmark)
      "Networks in Research Practice and Content."
   Thomas Sanders, U.S. Naval Academy (U.S.)
      "Encounter-ing World History: Thoughts on a World History Research Agenda from a Recent Collaborative Project."
   Esperanza Brizuela-Garcia, Upper Montclair State University (U.S.) & **Martin Valadez**, Stanford University (U.S.)
      "World History and Histories from the World."
   Tiffany Trimmer, Bowling Green State University (U.S.)
      "(Another) Call for World Historical Analysis of Networks and Networked Institutions."
   J. B. "Jack" Owens, Idaho State University (U.S.)
      "The Complex, Self-organizing Networks of the First Global Age (1400-1800): A high priority for world historical research."
   Laurie Schmitt, Friends' Central School (U.S.)
      "Perspectives on Peace."

12:00 AM – 2:00 PM: Session 7 — Concluding Session
   Moderator: Patrick Manning, University of Pittsburgh (U.S.)

GLOBAL PRACTICE IN WORLD HISTORY

Notes

1. Conference materials online include the Call for Proposals, conference program, conference statements of one thousand words from each presenter, biographic summaries for presenters, list of conference committee members and observers, the conference transcript, and a conference summary. This chapter is a revised and updated version of the conference summary posted on the conference website in January 2007. www.worldhistorynetwork.org/dev/conference.htm.
2. Patrick Manning, Transcript, 2:154. References to the "Transcript" are to the two text files of the transcribed record of the conference that have been made available to all participants at www.worldhistorynetwork.org/dev/conference.htm.
3. Transcript, 1:1–2.
4. Call for papers: www.worldhistorynetwork.org/dev/conference.htm.
5. Conference statements by Jerome Teelucksingh, Zhang Weiwei, Debin Ma, John E. Wills, Jr., Ali Çaksu, Potukuchi Swarnalatha, and Adapa Satyanarayana. Conference statements are available at the conference website, www.worldhistorynetwork.org/dev/conference. Jerome Teelucksingh submitted his statement, but was unable to attend the conference.
6. Esperanza Brizuela-Garcia, Transcript 2:138–142; Tiffany Trimmer, Transcript 2:137–138.
7. David Perry, Transcript, 1:250. Only four of thirty-six presenters appear to work on eras before 1500.
8. Transcript, 1:24–5.
9. Transcript, 2:56–7.
10. Conference statements by Marnie Hughes-Warrington, Libby Robin and Will Steffen, Kathleen Kimball, David Christian. Libby Robin and Will Steffen submitted their statement, but were unable to attend the conference.
11. Transcript, 1:11–15.
12. Conference statements by Laurie Schmitt, Hans-Heinrich Nolte, John Richards, Ingo Heidbrink, Roger Beck, David Lindenfeld, and Kathleen Kimball. John Richards submitted his statement but was unable to attend the conference.
13. Conference statements by Boris Stremlin, Katja Naumann and Matthias Middell, Leslie Witz, Sylvia Pappe, Marnie Hughes-Warrington, Potukuchi Swarnalatha, Adapa Satyanarayana.
14. Transcript, 1:47–8.
15. Adapa, Transcript, 2:4–5, asks why world history studies of migration (and reverse migration) in Asia focus so little on intra-Asian migrations.
16. Stremlin, Transcript, 1:25–7.
17. Dipesh Chakrabarty, *Provincializing Europe: Postcolonial Thought and Historical Difference* (Princeton: Princeton University Press, 2000).
18. Carol A. Breckenridge et al., eds., *Cosmopolitanism* (Durham: Duke University Press, 2002); and Kwame Anthony Appiah, *Cosmopolitanism: Ethics in a World of Strangers* (New York: Norton, 2007).
19. Conference statements by Annette Skovsted Hansen, Tiffany Trimmer, and J. G. Owens. See also Transcript, 2:52–3, 77–8, and 104–6, but note the caution in Transcript, 2:109, and Stremlin's reminder that states, too, are networks (Transcript, 2:112).
20. Peter Gran, Transcript, 1:24.
21. Martin Valadez, Transcript, 2:144.
22. Howard Spodek, Transcript, 1:65–66.

23. Manning and Owens, Transcript, 1:59–63.
24. Beck and Lindenfeld (Transcript 2:182) announced an initiative to form a group of world historians studying religion in world history.
25. Conference statements by Ralph Croizier and Kimball.
26. Conference statement by Nolte.
27. Conference statement by Schmitt.
28. Conference statements by Perry and Spodek.
29. Conference statement by Robin and Steffen.
30. Conference statement by George Dehner.
31. Conference statement by Heidbrink.
32. Conference statement by Richards.
33. Conference statement by Anne Chao.
34. Conference statement by Roland Wenzlhuemer.
35. Conference statements by Cyrus Veeser, Debin Ma, and Ingo Koponen.
36. Transcript, 1:79–82, 85, 90–91.
37. Conference statements by Marilyn Lake, Anne Gerritsen, Peter Adebayo, Thomas Sanders, Esperanza Brizuela-Garcia, Adapa, Trimmer, Perry, and Spodek.
38. Hughes-Warrington, Transcript, 1:40.
39. Heather Streets, Transcript, 1:160–161; Lake, Transcript 1:166; Sanders, Transcript 2:82–83.
40. Transcript, 1:57, 64, 76–77, 99.
41. Conference statement by Robin and Steffen; Transcript, 1: 4–5.
42. Conference statements by Trimmer, Owens, Sanders, and Ma. Ma reports that he is already engaged in a large collaborative project collecting economic data; Owens proposes the development of still larger historical databases, relying on Geographic Information Systems (GIS) technology.
43. Hansen, Transcript, 2:76–79.
44. Perry, Transcript, 2:20.
45. As Kathleen Kimball pointed out, if we lack written records for the Paleolithic, we have lots of visual records, reaching back at least 50,000 years. Transcript, 1:140. However, using that evidence will require forms of training (in visual literacy for example) that few world historians possess at present.
46. For instance, the Cambridge and international baccalaureate diploma programs of pre-university level .
47. "*AHR* Conversation on Transnational History," *American Historical Review*, 111 (2006): 1445.
48. Numerous overviews, manuals, and exemplary works have appeared in the various fields of study exceeding national boundaries. On transnational history: Akira Iriye, "Transnational History," *Contemporary European History* 13 (2004): 211–222; and Ann Curthoys and Marilyn Lake, eds., *Connected Worlds: History in Transnational Perspective* (Canberra: ANU Press, 2006). On global history: A. G. Hopkins, ed., *Global History: Interactions between the Universal and the Local* (London: Palgrave Macmillan, 2005); and Pamela Kyle Crossley, *What is Global History?* (Cambridge: Polity Press, forthcoming 2008). On new global history: Bruce Mazlish, New Global History (London: Routledge, 2006). On imperial history: Kathleen Wilson, ed., *A New Imperial History: Culture, Identity and Modernity in Britain and the Empire, 1660–1840* (Cambridge: Cambridge University Press, 2004). On international history: Marc Trachtenberg, *The Craft of International History* (Princeton: Princeton University Press, 2006).

On big history: David Christian, *Maps of Time: An Introduction to Big History* (Berkeley: University of California Press, 2004). On world history: Patrick Manning, *Navigating World History: Historians Create a Global Past* (New York: Palgrave Macmillan, 2003); Marnie Hughes-Warrington, ed., *Palgrave Advances in World Histories* (London: Palgrave Macmillan, 2005); and Patrick Manning, ed., *World History: Global and Local Interactions* (Princeton: Markus Wiener, 2005).

49. For some specific distinctions between approaches in transnational history and world history, see Ann Curthoys and Marilyn Lake, "Introduction," in Curthoys and Lake, *Connected Worlds*, 5–19; and Tony Ballantyne, "Putting the Nation in its Place? World History and C. A. Bayly's *The Birth of the Modern World*," in ibid., 20–43.
50. Transcript, 1:146.
51. Christian, Transcript, 2:69–70.
52. Christian, Transcript, 1:263–264.
53. For example, Gerritsen, Transcript, 2:13–16; and Spodek, Transcript, 2:27, on the city as a powerful way of linking the global and the local. But see also the caution from Leslie Witz, Transcript, 2:34, and the following discussion, Transcript, 2:34–49.
54. William Clarence-Smith and Christian, Transcript, 2:110–111; Benedict Anderson, Imagined Communities: Reflections on the Origin and Spread of Nationalism, rev. ed. (New York: Verso, 1991).
55. The German mathematician, David Hilbert (1862–1943), is widely regarded as one of the most influential mathematicians of the twentieth century. He was particularly concerned to think through the foundations of his discipline. In 1900, at the International Congress of Mathematicians held in Paris, he proposed a famous list of 23 (originally 24) fundamental problems facing the discipline. This list has shaped mathematical research ever since. One hundred years later 9 of Hilbert's problems had been solved, another 8 had been partially solved, and some had been shown to be insoluble as originally formulated.
56. That scholarship has been thoroughly reviewed in Manning, *Navigating World History*.
57. Manning, personal communication.
58. Conference statement by Hughes-Warrington. On the inclusion of Asia, Africa, and the Caribbean, see the conference statements of Adapa, Swarnalatha, Brizuela-Garcia, and Teelucksingh..
59. Stremlin, Transcript, 1:248.
60. Transcript, 2:161–162.
61. www.fas.harvard.edu/~chgis/.
62. Transcript, 2: 31, and 163–164.
63. Transcript, 2:151.
64. Streets and Lindenfeld, Transcript, 2:158–159, 185–186.
65. For instance, since doctoral programs in the UK and some other countries emphasize research almost to the exclusion of coursework, there is concern about how students will get adequate preparation for world-historical research within the time available. Transcript, 2: 176–177.
66. Conference statement by Owens.
67. Transcript, 1:5–6.
68. Lake, Transcript, 2:204–205.
69. Dehner, Transcript, 1:74–75.

CHAPTER 2

Monographic and Macro Histories: Confronting Paradigms

Diego Olstein

The teaching of world history at The Hebrew University of Jerusalem resulted from a profound institutional innovation: the founding of the School of History. The aim of the School of History is to provide a framework for all historians and students dispersed among the history departments (History, History of the Jewish People, and Art History) and the regional-studies departments (Islamic and Middle East Studies, African Studies, East Asian Studies, Russian and Slavic Studies, American Studies, Spanish and Latin American Studies, and Indian, Iranian and Armenian Studies). This inclusiveness is possible for two reasons. First, these fields share the basic principles of the historical discipline and, second, the School of History emphasizes the transcendence of the regional boundaries toward an all-encompassing unit of analysis—the world. This new organizational mode has affected the program of study in the above-mentioned departments and diverse academic activities at several levels: the teaching of a core-course curriculum and seminars, inter-departmental collaboration, international meetings, university-community relations, and world-history research.

One significant achievement of the School of History is an introductory course on world history given to students from all the above-mentioned departments. Two models inform the introductory courses on world history—a narrative-synthetic model and an analytical model. The narrative-synthetic course consists of an introductory survey structured according to five main principles: four fundamental types of societies (nomadic, agricultural, maritime, and industrial); two major transformations in economies (the agricultural and Industrial revolutions); two major intellectual transformations (the axial age and the scientific revolution); two fundamental types of political regimes (the command system and the market system); and four scales of spatial integration (multiple regional systems, the Indian-basin system, the Atlantic-basin system, and globalization).

In the analytical course, the units of teaching are thematically arranged. The course provides a cross-section of world history by dividing the field of study according to key issues: environment, time and space, demography, economics, social structures, political regimes, warfare and conquest, cultural contacts, and cosmologies.

The introductory course on world history is not the only result of inter-departmental collaboration. Also an inter-departmental advanced seminar on monographic and macro histories resulted from this collaboration. This chapter presents the highlights of the seminar in two senses. Explicitly, this chapter summarizes the main contents and conclusions of the seminar. The contents and conclusions concern the different conceptual paths of macro history—world history, world-system approach, civilizational analysis, historical sociology, and comparative history—and the specific relationship between those paths and the monographic history written by area-studies experts.[1] Implicitly, beyond the specific contents, the chapter presents a model of world-history teaching for advanced students. The teaching model consists of two basic components: a) the gathering of scholars from different macro-historical disciplines and several area studies, and b) the arrangement of the seminar discussions along a unifying organizing principle.

Macro History and Area Studies: Confronting Paradigms

The interdisciplinary seminar departed from a large-scale mapping of the historical discipline, which makes a clear-cut distinction between two realms of historical writing: monographic and macro-historical. The emergence of history as an academic field is closely related to the consolidation of the modern nation-state. For this reason, and as a result of institutional and ideological constraints, historians have generally adopted the nation-state (and the political entities preceding it) as the basic unit of analysis, making the study of history a monographic enterprise. The subsequent emergence of regional-area studies was shaped by a similar conception, although non-nation-state criteria (language, religion, and culture, for example) defined the unit of analysis. Moreover, the monographic conception has persisted almost untouched in the research and writing of history in all the historiographical approaches that have evolved since the last quarter of the nineteenth century. Economic, social, cliometric, intellectual, cultural, gender-based, and post-colonial branches of historical knowledge essentially assumed that the nation-state, or another enclosed unit, was the undisputed unit of analysis. However, a wide range of historical fields directly challenges the perennial unit of analysis by transcending the nation-states or other borders: world history, comparative history, civilization analysis, world systems, and historical sociology. For these macro-historical approaches, the crossing of boundaries is indispensable for the process of historical inquiry, given that it adopts a new unit of analysis: the world, or a significant part of it, rather than the nation-state, its preceding political entities, or another kind of enclosed unit. Relying on this major contrast between monographic histories (in which area studies are included) and macro histories, the first part of the seminar was dedicated to an analysis of the variety of macro histories. Once the macro-historical realm was mapped out, we examined the ways in which macro histories and monographic area studies potentially and actually communicate.

The Range of Macro Histories: The Substantial-Analytical Rift

Crossing of national boundaries being the major shared feature of macro histories, the way in which each macro-history transcends these boundaries defines the main differences between them. National boundaries can be transcended either analytically or substantially. Comparative history transcends the boundaries analytically by studying the shared and different features of a particular phenomenon, process, or institution in two or more units enclosed by national boundaries. This procedure derives from the basic aim of comparative history—making contrasts between units. World history is different. Given that its main purpose is to connect units, world history transcends the boundaries substantially by focusing on phenomena – the impact, contacts, links, integration, diffusion, and migration from one unit to another—that transcend national boundaries. Also, world-historical units of analysis are usually larger than those of comparative history and include—in addition to nation-states or regions—continents, ocean basins, hemispheres, and the entire world. Similarly, analysis based on civilizations deals with large units of analysis, indeed the whole world. Once again, this is the result of the concrete transcending of borders, with civilization-based traits being a cross-national-borders phenomenon. However, on the other hand, the definition of civilizations is obtained by contrasting these huge compartmentalized units. Therefore, the transcendence of these new and larger boundaries is analytical in the same way as comparative history. A particular interest in encounters and conflicts between civilizations brings civilizational analysis closer to world history, which, as a result of its analytical and contrastive features, is otherwise much more closely related to comparative history.

Another field akin to comparative history is historical sociology. To begin with, the transcendence of national boundaries is analytical and its aim is contrastive. Its singularity, however, results from its profound aspiration for generalization, which is lacking in comparative history. By means of contrasting the enclosed units, it targets the necessary and sufficient conditions of a particular phenomenon, such as the rise of the modern state, modernization, and dictatorship. The world-system approach, which focuses on cross-border phenomena, such as capital accumulation, world division of labor, and struggle for political hegemony, transcends the national boundaries substantially. Therefore, as in the case of world history, the prevailing unit of analysis is the world as a whole.

Crossing the borders analytically to make a contrast, or crossing them substantially for the sake of linking, is, therefore, the major divide within the macro-histories realm. Moreover, a concomitant series of assumptions follow, reinforcing and emphasizing this primary divide. These assumptions relate to the space and time dimensions and the formulation of causal relations. The macro histories that transcend the national borders analytically—comparative history, civilization analysis, and historical sociology—assume that the units under comparison are self-enclosed. Given that the space dimension is composed of enclosed units of analysis, the historian is able to select for comparison different units from the entire time span. In this sense, a diachronic definition of time dimension is privileged. In addition, a further assumption might be drawn from the primacy of a diachronic definition of time, whereby each singular unit follows its own periodization and evolves along its own specific path. With each unit being enclosed and transiting its own historical path, the causation of processes is endogenous. In contrast, a substantial crossing of borders brings about an integrated rather than a compartmentalized world. Defining space as the globe as whole, the actions/processes taking place at a single point/period in time all across the world—real time—are of greater importance. Therefore, a synchronic view of time prevails. This view might lead to a single periodization that rules the entire globe. Although the causation of processes proceeds within the integrated whole, from the compartmentalized perspective, causation is exogenous.

Table 1. Classifying the Wide Range of Macro Histories: The Substantial-Analytical Rift

DEFINING FEATURES	MACRO HISTORIES	
	World History World-system Approach Civilization Analysis	Comparative History Historical Sociology Civilization Analysis
Way of Transcending National Boundaries	Substantially	Analytically
Space Dimension: The Basic Units of Analysis	The World as Ultimate Unit of Analysis	Several Enclosed Units (Nation-state/Civilization)
Time Dimension	Synchronic	Diachronic
Causality Attribution	Exogenous	Endogenous

The above oversimplified scheme was designed to map the differences within macro histories. Nevertheless, the parsimony of this scheme should not hide the considerable variance of historiography that exists within each macro-historical enterprise. To begin with the analytical border crossers, *comparative history* contains a wide variety of research designs to pursue different aims: explanation of uniqueness, formulation of generalizations, and depiction of varieties within a pattern. Each of these designs is related to a particular method of comparison: crucial agreement/difference, deductive or parallel comparison, and concomitant variation in correspondence. The framework of *civilizational analysis* can be divided into four sections by dealing with two crucial antinomies. The first is the antinomy of material (geographic, economic) versus ideal (structures of consciousness, imaginary signification) variables as primary criteria for the definition of civilizations. The second is the antinomy of the same general divide between macro histories: a comparative study of civilization patterns and their historical trajectories versus the decisive role of interaction and inter-civilization encounters. Because of this internal fracture, civilization analysis belongs to either the analytical or substantial border crossers.

Historical sociology encompasses two major agendas, each stressing one of the components of its name. The first strategy is initially historical and only afterwards sociological. It identifies recurrent structures and sequences across time and space to depict patterns. Another aim is to inform human choices in the present and future while dealing with historical problems persisting into the present. The second approach operates from the opposite direction, by applying sociological conclusions derived from the study of contemporary societies to the past.

In the realm of the substantial border crossers, several sub-categories may be depicted. The rich harvest of *world-history* studies of the last fifteen years may be classified according to their object of study. The resulting typology entails four categories: the history of time units, space units, variables (economics, ecology, demography, gender, culture, and politics), and processes (evolution, contacts, and diffusion). Conversely, each of these categories includes studies using different scales, ranging from the widest to the narrowest (for example, time units, from millennia to one year; space units, from the entire planet to a single village; and variables, from world economy to a specific commodity).[2] Finally, the main division within the *world-system approach* is chronology and its underlying assumptions. Is the world system five hundred or five thousand years old (with several possibilities in between)? The answer to this question determines the geographical scope of the system as well as its defining features.

Having said this, we should not push these differences, significant as they might be, too far.[3] Even before the emergence of world history as a distinctive historical perspective, Hodgson had already noted its problematic relationship with comparative history. In an article dedicated to the conditions of historical comparison, he stressed the importance of the relationship in which each compared unit was involved with its region (for example, although both Vikings and Polynesians engaged in exploration, the former were part of a wider configuration—the Oikoumene—while the latter were isolated).[4] This preliminary suggestion has become a key in the attempts made in recent years to adjust the analytical and substantial procedures. McMichael has provided a second key by defining the "incorporated comparison." Instead of juxtaposing several units, this type of historical comparison adopts connected and mutually conditioning processes as its subject of comparison.[5] In recent years, several works of comparative world history containing one of these two orientations have evolved. Pomeranz applies the first principle, in his book *The Great Divergence*, in which he selects for comparison parts of his units—Europe, China, Japan, and India—which are similarly positioned within their worlds. From the global perspective, he is able to make comparisons between two parts of the whole and observe how their position and function within it shapes their nature.[6] The recent historical research on globalization resembles the second path of combination. In this case, the same worldwide process is compared at two chronological stages: the last part of the twentieth century and the second half of the nineteenth century, or "today's globalization" and the "first great globalization" of 1850–1914.[7]

In brief, as a result of its own historicity, modern historiography emerged and developed as a monographic enterprise. Nevertheless, several globalizing conditions inspired a number of macro-historical enterprises ready to cross the traditional borders challenging the unquestioned nation-state unit of analysis. Crossing these borders analytically or substantially implied opposing assumptions: enclosed versus integrated space, diachronic versus synchronic time, and endogenous versus exogenous causation. Despite this clear divide, by concentrating on the functional relationship of the enclosed units in comparison to the world as a whole, or by comparing a world process at different historical stages, we could profit from the combination of the procedures transcending the boundaries both analytically and substantially. Moreover, beyond the internal dialogue among macro histories, the deepest challenge lays in combining the meticulous depth of monographic history with the widest breadth of macro history. In our seminar, this challenge was applied to the history of Asia.

Macro Histories and Area Studies: Six Paths for Enrichment and Debate

The second part of the seminar confronted macro histories with area studies. The discussions were arranged according to the regional criterion embedded both in area studies and civilizational analysis. The following is an exposition, also arranged by regions, of the existing ways of communication between monographic histories and macro histories, and some suggestions for future attempts to connect the two.

Ancient Mesopotamia: an impressive feedback cycle. The main division within the *world-system approach* is based on chronology. The earliest stage proposed for the emergence of the world system coincides with the appearance of civilization in Mesopotamia. In this region, it is claimed, the complex and hierarchical societies that emerged were integrated by using networks in which important, two-way, ordinary interaction linked peoples, creating a world system. As such, the space was arranged along a scheme of strong core polities and weaker and dependent peripheral societies, with semi-peripheral societies in the middle. Moreover, being a world system, its time-span evolved in cyclical patterns: urban and empire growth and decline and expansion and contraction of trade networks influenced by climate change. The first two cycles discussed are Uruk expansion and the Akkadian Empire. Uruk expansion was accomplished, as described in the seminar, by founding colonies and colonial enclaves within existing towns across a vast region to gain access to desired goods and to control trade routes. The Akkadian Empire is considered the first instance of a core-wide empire resulting from the conquest of a number of older core-states.

Back to the world system chronological divide, for those that define the world system as a modern phenomenon exclusively, neither the Uruk nor the Akkadian Empire fit the world-system definition. Either because of their incapability to project military power far from its borders or because they lacked elaborated capitalistic mechanisms for facilitating unequal exchange, both the Uruk and the Akkadian Empire were unable to extract resources from distant peripheral areas. However, the most interesting contact lies not within the world-system approach. By contrasting paradigms, we find an impressive feedback cycle between the world-system approach and monographic research. Unsurprisingly, the first stage of this dialogue is the extensive reliance of world-system literature on Ancient Mesopotamia on monographic research in this area.[8] The second stage results from the previous stage: a fruitful synthesis of large quantities of very specific focused articles that provide a comprehensive overview.[9] The third stage of the dialogue, the truly surprising one, turns the feedback full circle. Monographic research is inspired by, referred to, and even manifested in the analytical framework of the world-system approach.[10]

Muslim Middle East: two roads to macro histories. The formation and consolidation of Islam took place through a series of border-crossing processes: military conquest, language diffusion, religious conversion, pilgrimage, long-distance trade, and agricultural and technological transfers. These types of processes are the very subjects with which world history deals. Therefore, both Middle East studies and world history have shared a common ground from the outset. Moreover, as these foundational processes unfolded, they created a "Muslim Commonwealth," a "Muslim World System." In this sense, a new road of communication is opened, this time between Middle East studies and the world-system approach. Here, the world-system conceptual framework can contribute in articulating monographic research so that it provides a comprehensive view of the Muslim Middle East.

This foundational stage of Islam was followed by manifold interactions between the Muslim Middle East and its multiple neighboring societies—Europe, Africa, India, and China, but first and foremost with the peoples from the Steppes of Central Asia. These are subjects for world history at its best. To put it briefly, we see from a list of major subjects in Muslim Middle East studies that this field is open to macro histories through an internal road, dealing also with its foundational processes and its resulting outcome, and an external road for the subsequent interregional contacts.

Central Asia: a marvelous case of correspondence. By definition, world history is a macro-historical enterprise that transcends boundaries substantially. The history of Central Asia is that of nomadic societies whose existence was structurally conditioned to cross borders. To a large extent, therefore, Central Asia's history is world history. This has been the case from the period of the Hsiung-Nu expansion to the Timurid states, and through the Turkish Qaganates and the Mongol Empire. All these developments involved a pattern of conquest by pastoral nomadic confederations of tribes. However, the Mongol expansion and empire epitomized this trend by their synthesis of two different traditions – the Steppes empires based in the Mandate of Heaven ideology and the

Manchurian peoples that maintained nomadic rule over large agricultural societies, and by invigorating these traditions with innovations such as military-unit organization, transfer of populations, direct taxation, and a riding post service.

This initial correspondence between world history and Central Asia, both of which are based on transcending boundaries, contains a confluence of interests that seals their close affinity. Among the aims of world history are inclusion of "peoples without history," visualization of new perspectives, and a new balance between the world's regions. The concern for "peoples without history" by world historians is part of their interest in pastoral nomadic societies. One of the new perspectives developed by world historians that challenge the linear succession of "hunter-gatherer/farmer/industrial societies" is the long-lasting interactions between sedentary and nomadic societies. A new balance of regional attention, in which Central Asia is better positioned, takes shape. As a result, these three features bring world history very close to the perspective of Central Asia studies. Simultaneously, Central Asia studies, being a region on the move and dependent on its surrounding neighbors, are a receptive field for the insights provided by world history.

India: instructive contrast. The crucial contrast that emerged from the confrontation of world history and area studies regarding the history of India is geographic. Simply stated, to world historians, India means northern India. By contrast, area studies, which seek to capture pristine India, target the southern part of the subcontinent. These preferences are understandable given the biases derived from each perspective. With world history being a substantial border-crossing field of study, it is natural to stress the intermittent contacts, conquests, and migrations that have dotted Indian history and arose, or were consolidated, in the north. Thus, world-history books depict the history of India as a succession of migrations and conquests from the time of the Aryans' invasion to the time of the Indian Empire. Monographic research, on the other hand, aims at the local, the idiosyncratic, and the unique, so it focuses on South India because of its detachment from the recurrent foreign intrusions. Contrary to the imperial history of northern India, which roughly synchronized with successive empires elsewhere in Asia, monographic history, through the experience of the southern part of the subcontinent, provides a singular characterization of Indian political history. Distant from the imperial history of the north, the outstanding feature of southern political history is the weakness of the state that resulted from the rift between the power of the king and the authority of the Brahmins. Moreover, the realm of power underwent a process of "de-ontologization," i.e., the power sphere became irrelevant in crucial existential matters. Rather, the spiritual realm, which the Brahmins control, is most important. However, despite the geographical split between world and monographic histories at this point, an interesting intersection appears when addressing state formation in the south. For instance, Stein's model on the consolidation of the Vijayanagara kingdom (from 1340 to its crisis in the late sixteenth century) as a prototype of the future regimes in the south closely recalls the widely-known model of absolutist/gunpowder empires. Here as elsewhere, military innovations created a financial need that was provided by a shift in agriculture toward cash crops, monetization of the economy, and urbanization.[11] The contrast here between macro and monographic histories is enlightening in two ways. First, by pursuing different objectives—border crossing or enclosure—macro histories and monographic histories can complement each other. Second, no matter how idiosyncratic a case appears to be, it is helpful to be acquainted with the general patterns reconstructed by macro histories that might rest underneath uniqueness.

China: reconciling comparative and systemic views. Monographic histories on China rely heavily on comparative crucial difference, with two central phenomena at play: success and stagnation. Success is reflected by enduring political and cultural continuity, stagnation by economic decay. Success is explained by the stability provided by the special gentry-bureaucracy relationship, Confucianism, imperial restraint, and moral economy. Stagnation, too, is explained by stability, in this case technological stability. Its result, the "high-level equilibrium trap," enabled quantitative growth that subsequently resulted in a qualitative standstill. Diminishing returns and Malthusian dynamics have fostered economic decay since the late eighteenth century. Europe, with its fragmented political history and economic growth, is the implicit unit in making this comparison, from which China's uniqueness emerged.

Surprisingly, however, stressing uniqueness to the limit creates an affinity with macro histories. China's uniqueness relies on its precocious political, cultural, and economic integration. Moreover, its achievements took place in a huge area. This intersection—large-scale political, cultural, and economic integration—provides a basis for considering Chinese history as a world-system history. Similarly, these features compel the inclusion of Chinese history in the conceptual framework of globalization. Therefore, an explicit comparative approach should be designed in trying to understand China's strengths and failures. Doing so would overcome the distinction between analytical and substantial macro histories in the twofold way discussed above. On the one hand, we could compare China as a particular world system to another world system, as Chase-Dunn has done for ten different types of world systems. Similarly, the globalization taking place in China could be viewed in the framework of comparative globalization. On the other hand, "incorporated comparisons," which take into account the relationship of each unit with its region and the mutually-conditioning processes in which all of the units are immersed, might by applied as well. Indeed, recent studies, such as the work of Kenneth Pomeranz, have moved in this direction.

Japan: linked by a concept. Diffusion, an important concept shared by Japanese-area studies and world history, fruitfully linked the two disciplines. Through long diffusion processes, Japan was presented first as a variant of China and then as a variant of the West. In both cases, its geographical location enabled Japan to impede the influx of foreign influence. For centuries, Japan relied on Chinese inputs for the development of its economy and culture. Rice cultivation, irrigation systems, metalwork, production of textiles (including silk and dyeing), and patterns of urbanization are fundamental economic elements that Japan inherited from China. In the cultural sphere, the Japanese adopted Chinese as its learned language. Not only did this result in the adoption of the Japanese writing system, it also enabled the Japanese to acquire the sciences (astronomy, medicine, and mathematics), historiography, social and political philosophy (Confucianism), and jurisprudence that developed in China. Also, Buddhism entered Japan via China, as did forms of religious art (temples, sculptures, and paintings). In all these cases, however, the Japanese carried out a deliberate selection and adaptation process.

During the sixteenth century, a new avenue of diffusion became available for Japan. The Portuguese Jesuit mission converted a half million Japanese (out of a population of twenty-five million) to Christianity. The mission's success was a Pyrrhic victory: Japan expelled the Jesuits and closed the country to outside influence in 1636, except for the Dutch colony that was allowed to remain as a trading post. Here, too, the language was first learned by scholars commissioned by the Shogun. Books from Holland followed and with them came western science (astronomy, medicine, and mathematics). Ultimately, as we know, the overwhelming Western influence arrived much later, after 1853. Since then, the Western model has informed Japan's economy and culture: industrialization and urbanization, a constitution and a parliament. In daily life, too, Western influence has replaced Chinese influence. This is evident in the clothes, hairstyles, calendar, gastronomy, and the like. Conversely, by switching to the Western source of influence, Japan entered the regional and world scene while initiating its own imperialist design and stamping a major imprint on world history.

Conclusions

A clear-cut typology of macro histories emerged from the first part of the seminar: substantial or analytical border-crossing fields. The second part of the seminar generated two primary ways of communication, with different intensity, between Asian studies and macro histories. On the one hand, there is a mode of viable links, which stimulates feedback, congruence, and correspondence. On the other hand, a contrastive mode stressing uniqueness communicates more hesitantly. These two modes of communication between area studies and macro histories seem to be related to both the conspicuous historical features of each area investigated and to the defining assumptions of each macro-historical field. In this way, areas characterized as spaces in movement, such as the Middle East and Central Asia, favored the substantial border-crossing type of macro-history. Conversely, China's history, which is primarily conceived as internal history, is more prone to the analytical border-crossing type of macro histories. In between lay the cases of India and Japan. India's northern part is characterized by intermittent movements that bring it close to world history, while its more closed southern part bears an affinity with analytic macro histories. In Japan studies, predominant interest lies in internal history, making it closer to analytical macro histories, while recognition of the importance of external diffusion in the development of this inner history brings the analysis closer to substantial macro histories.

Table 2. All Together Now: Area Studies and Macro Histories

Area-studies Perspectives	Inner History	Spaces on the Move
Macro Histories	Analytical	Substantial
Communication Mode	Contrastive	Correspondent
Cases	China South India Japan	Middle East, Central Asia North India Japan

Whatever the mode of communication, the confrontation of area studies and macro histories was highly encouraging and instructive. Firstly, on the content side, mapping the realm of macro histories enhanced the search for ways of collaboration between them. Moreover the seminar, in response to its primary aim, corroborated that historical research should proceed at both monographic and macro levels simultaneously. Finally, regarding the teaching model, this first seminar was arranged according to the regional criterion embedded both in area studies and civilizational analysis. However, an entire series of "confrontation seminars" of this type can be developed by arranging each of them pursuant to the criteria of another macro-historical field. Given that world history is the organizing key, area-studies experts from areas engaged in a particular trans-boundaries phenomenon will be engaged, along with macro-historians, in a "multilateral" approach. The adoption of a world-system perspective will help integrate regional processes into a coherent whole. Comparisons grounded in sound scholarship could be the outcome of a comparative "confrontation seminar," and several patterns could be tracked globally in an historical-sociological seminar. These "confrontation seminars," therefore, offer a fruitful and wide teaching framework. Moreover, by eroding the old monographic categories and by fostering new networks of scholarly interaction, they might inspire macro-historical research as well.

Notes

1. For a complete account on the teaching of world history teaching at The Hebrew University, Jerusalem, see D. Olstein, "World History: An Integrative Model," *World History Bulletin*, 20, 2 (2004): 4–6. The list of contributors to the seminar includes S. N. Eisenstadt (Civilization Analysis), Y. Harari (World History), D. Olstein (World System, Comparative History, and Historical Sociology), N. Wasserman (Ancient Mesopotamia), A. David (Ancient Egypt), R. Amitai (Medieval Islam), E. Ginio (Ottoman Empire), M. Biran (Central Asia in the Middle Ages), R. Sela (Early Modern Central Asia), D. Shulman (India), Y. Pines (China), and B. Shillony (Japan).
2. For a typology of world history writing, see D. Olstein, "La nueva historia mundial en sus variedades," *Actas del III Congreso Internacional Historia a Debate* (Santiago de Compostela: Historia a Debate Editorial, 2006).
3. D. Olstein, "Comparative History and World History: Contrasts and Contacts," in I. Shagrir, R. Ellenblum, and J. Riley-Smith, eds., *In Laudem Hierosolymitani: Studies in Crusades and Medieval Culture in Honour of Benjamin Z. Kedar* (Aldershot, UK: Ashgate, 2006).
4. M. Hodgson, "Conditions of Historical Comparison among Ages and Regions," in E. Burke, ed., *Rethinking World History: Essays on Europe, Islam, and World History* (Cambridge: Cambridge University Press, 1993), 267–27.
5. P. McMichael, "Incorporating Comparison within a World-Historical Perspective: An Alternative Comparative Method," *American Sociological Review* 55 (1990): 385–397.
6. K. Pomeranz, *The Great Divergence: China, Europe, and the Making of the Modern World Economy* (Princeton, NJ: Princeton University Press, 2000).
7. D. Olstein, "The Multiple Origins of Globalization: Examining Conceptual Issues," *Contemporanea* 3 (2006).
8. For examples of monographic research that informs world-system analysis, see R. Adams and N. Hans, *The Uruk Countryside* (Chicago: University of Chicago Press, 1972); and J. S. Cooper, "Sumerian and Akkadian in Sumer and Akkad," in G. Buccellati, ed., "Approaches to the Study of the Ancient Near East: A Volume of Studies Offered to Ignace J. Gelb," *Orientalia* 42 (1973): 239–246.
9. For examples of world-system overviews on Ancient Mesopotamia, see M. Allen, "The Mechanisms of Underdevelopment: An Ancient Mesopotamian Example," Review 15 (1992): 453-476; and C. Cioffi-Revilla, "War and politics in ancient Mesopotamia, 2900-539 BC: Measurement and Comparative Analysis," *LORANOW Project* (Boulder: University of Colorado, 1995).
10. For examples of monographic research inspired by, referred to, and manifested in the analytic framework of the world system approach, see G. Algaze, *The Uruk World System: The Dynamics of Expansion of Early Mesopotamian Civilization* (Chicago: University of Chicago Press, 1993); and G. Stein, *Rethinking World Systems: Diasporas, Colonies, and Interaction in Uruk Mesopotamia* (Tucson: University of Arizona Press, 1999).
11. B. Stein, *The New Cambridge History of India*, Vol. I.2. *Vijayanagara* (Cambridge: Cambridge University Press, 1993).

CHAPTER 3

World History from an Islamic Perspective: The Experience of the International Islamic University Malaysia

Ahmed Ibrahim Abushouk

The contemporary call for Islamization of knowledge is a revivalist response to modernity and its secular impact on Muslim society and educational institutions. It stems from the premise that contemporary knowledge is neither value-free nor universal, but it has been designed by Western scholars who frame the world from their own distinct cultural, historical and secular perspective. This call was popularized and developed by Ismail Raji al-Faruqi into a set of principles and work-plans that triggered a series of scholarly debates and discussions on the Islamic approach to knowledge and education.[1] This chapter attempts to examine the rationale of the Islamization of knowledge and its application at the International Islamic University Malaysia (IIUM) with a particular emphasis on the history and civilization programs that aim at encouraging students to cultivate an Islamic perspective through which they will be able to enhance their intellectual understanding of continuity and change in world history and civilizational dialogues across religions and nations.

The Rationale of Islamization of Knowledge

The idea of Islamization of knowledge began its formal journey sometime in 1977 CE/1397 AH, when the First World Conference on Muslim Education was held in Makkah at the invitation of King Abd al-Aziz University in Saudi Arabia. Around three hundred Muslim scholars attended the conference and discussed among other issues the need for the reform of the education system in the Muslim world and Islamization of knowledge.[2] Follow-up conferences and workshops were organized in other Muslim countries,[3] and notable institutions of academic caliber such as the International Institute of Islamic Thought (IIIT) joined the movement and promoted the Islamization of knowledge project. The Founding President of the IIIT, Ismail al-Faruqi, attributed the failure of the education system in the Muslim world to the lack of Islamic vision that would reflect Islamic ideals and synthesize Islamic values and legacy with the modern social sciences.[4] He then urged Muslim scholars to take up the task of reconstructing the order of knowledge in terms that were fundamentally Islamic, more culturally authentic and directly relevant to the contemporary needs of Muslims. Al-Faruqi's successor, Abdul Hamid AbuSulayman, traced the root causes of this problem to the crisis in the Muslim mind and a blind imitation of the West.[5] Both al-Faruqi and AbuSulayman departed from the presupposition that the body of secular knowledge in the West is neither as neutral nor as universal as some of its proponents claim it to be. They argue that the social sciences taught at Muslim universities are the products of this secular knowledge, and their methodologies, concepts, and explanations of human behavior and outlook on life and the universe are not in harmony with the fundamental teachings of Islam.[6] But at the same time they agree that these social sciences can be very important for the development of Muslim societies, if they are reformed in line with and made as an integral part of the Islamization of knowledge process.[7] In other words, the goal of the Islamization of knowledge project is "to redefine and reorder the data, to rethink the reasoning and relating of the data, to reevaluate the conclusions, to reproject the goals and to do so in such a way as to make the disciplines enrich the vision and serve the cause of Islam."[8] To achieve this goal, based on the systemic orientation and restructuring of the entire field of human knowledge, al-Faruqi identifies a set of epistemological principles, expressed in terms of five unities: the unity of God, the unity of creation, the unity of truth, the unity of life, and the unity of humanity.[9] He then embarks on a workplan comprising the following twelve steps:

1. Mastery of modern disciplines
2. Discipline survey
3. Mastery of Islamic legacy: the anthologies

4. Mastery of Islamic legacy: the analysis
5. Establishment of specific relevance of Islam to the disciplines
6. Critical assessment of the modern disciplines: the state of the art
7. Critical assessment of the Islamic legacy: the state of the art
8. Survey of the *ummah*'s major problems
9. Survey of the problems of humankind
10. Creative analysis and synthesis
11. Recasting the disciplines under the framework of Islam: the university textbooks
12. Dissemination of Islamized knowledge.[10]

This workplan aims at setting up a twofold movement of integration that requires the reconstruction of traditional Islamic and Western knowledge. In spite of its theoretical appeal, al-Faruqi's plan was criticized by some proponents of the Islamization of contemporary knowledge project, who doubted its practical viability and modified it into a simplified procedure based on the "mastery of substantive knowledge, mastery of methodological knowledge, and production of university text books."[11] They assumed that this modified version would effectively enable them to overcome the dichotomy between the modern secular and traditional Islamic systems of education, and produce an integral one.[12] Its implementation was entrusted to some newly established universities in the Muslim world, particularly the International Islamic University Malaysia.

International Islamic University Malaysia

The International Islamic University Malaysia (IIUM) was established in 1983 CE/1404 AH by the Malaysian Government with support from various Muslim countries and the Organization of the Islamic Conference (OIC). Its conception and development was inspired by the recommendations of the First World Conference on Muslim Education held in Makkah in 1977 CE /1397 AH, which called for the infusion of Islamic values in all aspects of education, including social sciences and humanities. Accordingly, the University aims at becoming an international center of educational excellence that seeks to restore the dynamic and progressive role of the Muslim ummah (nation) in all branches of knowledge. It also endeavors to introduce a unified teaching and learning process along with the inculcation of moral and spiritual values through "Integration, Islamization, Internationalization, and Comprehensive Excellence (IIICE)." The academic programs based on this vision are currently run by eleven faculties (known as kulliyyahs) and a few specialized centers.[13]

The Kulliyyah of Islamic Revealed Knowledge and Human Sciences (KIRKHS) in particular was established in 1990 CE/1411 AH, with ten departments (now eleven), as the heart of the Islamization of knowledge project. It presents "the reunification of theology, social sciences and humanities as envisaged in the Islamic world-view," so as to overcome the prevailing dichotomy between "religious" and "secular" disciplines.[14] The Kulliyyah is divided into two major divisions: 1. Islamic Revealed Knowledge and Heritage, and 2. Human Sciences. The first division consists of the Departments of Arabic Language and Literature, *Fiqh* and *Usul al-Fiqh* (Islamic Jurisprudence and Principles of Islamic Jurisprudence), Quran and Sunnah Studies, *Usuluddin* and Comparative Religion, and General Studies. The second division comprises the Departments of English Language and Literature, Communication, History and Civilization, Political Science, Psychology, and Sociology and Anthropology. Each department is designed to offer a Bachelor's degree in its major component with an elective package of courses in Islamic revealed knowledge and human science disciplines. The Bachelor's program in history and civilization, for example, leads to a Master of Human Sciences (M.HSc.) in History and Civilization that qualifies students to pursue their Doctorate program in the field.

Figure 1. Organization of KIRKHS (the Kulliyyah of Islamic Revealed Knowledge and Human Sciences at IIUM)

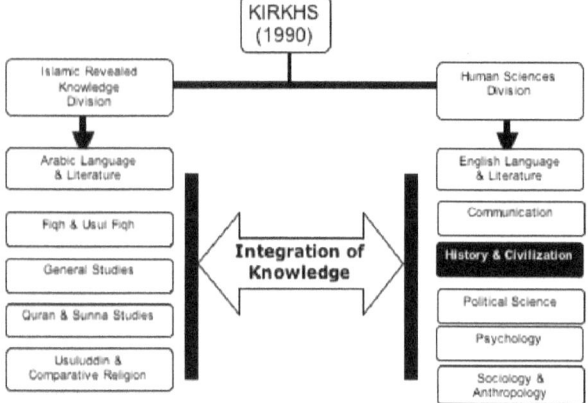

Department of History and Civilization

The Department of History and Civilization was established in 1990 CE/1411 AH as an independent academic unit within the Kulliyyah of Islamic Revealed Knowledge and Human Sciences (KIRKHS). It offers academic programs that serve the ultimate goal of the Kulliyyah, to integrate humanistic and religious knowledge in response to any social issues. These programs introduce students to the study of history and civilization from an Islamic perspective based on the revealed understanding of the causes and processes involved in the rise and fall of civilizations and in continuity and change in world history. The wide range of history and civilization courses offered by the department also provides professional training to students who wish to pursue their postgraduate studies in the field of history and civilization, or to seek careers as history teachers in secondary schools and colleges, archivists, museum officials, journalists, diplomats, and civil servants.[15]

Table 1. Growth of History and Civilization Students (2000–2005 CE/1421–1426 AH/).

Note that 1st to 4th levels refer to students in first to fourth year of their studies during each calendar year.

Year/ Semester	1st level	2nd level	3rd level	4th level	Total
2000/1	0	1	1	73	75
2000/2	0	1	1	70	72
2001/1	1	2	0	88	91
2001/2	1	2	0	88	91
2002/1	1	2	5	99	107
2002/2	2	3	7	99	111
2003/1	3	15	17	101	136
2003/2	2	20	22	93	137
2004/1	6	33	23	75	137
2004/2	9	36	23	67	135
2005/1	13	35	23	51	122
2005/2	13	36	23	34	106

The graduation statistical analysis shows that the Department of History and Civilization is one of the less popular departments of the Kulliyyah of Islamic Revealed Knowledge and Human Sciences. But here, I may argue that this statistic is not inclusive because it does not include history and civilization courses offered to non-history students. In the last the last five years, for example, the number of the students registered for history courses per semester (major, minor and elective) was consistently more than one thousand and five hundred students. The growth of those who majored in history and civilization is demonstrated in Table 1.

World History from an Islamic Perspective

The structure of the history and civilization curriculum was inspired by a number of studies on the interpretation of history from an Islamic perspective. The pioneer study in this respect is that of Abdul Hameed Siddiqi, "The Islamic Concept of History," presented at the First World Conference on Muslim Education.[16] In this paper, Siddiqi criticizes the Western concept of history which has completely eliminated revelation as a source of knowledge, thereby reducing it into the level of mere fiction and myth. He argues that this elimination has made it impossible for Muslim historians to incorporate revelation by relying on modern Western methodology. He, therefore, appealed to Muslim historians to develop a new universal view of history that would draw its principles from revelation, and to use traditional Islamic and Western research techniques to analyze historical events.

This appeal seems to have encouraged Syed Ali Ashraf, the first Secretary General of the Follow-up Committee of the First World Conference on Muslim Education, to produce a paper on "The Quranic Concept of History."[17] The paper focuses on the issue of the creation of human beings and argues that Adam was the first man on the earth and "a completely new creation endowed with spiritual knowledge and blessed with the duty of a Prophet for his children."[18] It rejects the Western concept that perceives the history of human beings from a gradual evolutionary perspective that had developed from primitiveness to modernity.[19] The author then maintains the understanding that,

> From Noah till the last Prophet there is a continuous line of Prophethood and human history, with the rise and fall of nations integrally related to faith and Man's behaviour, his acceptance or denial of the Message that Allah had sent through His prophets. Political authority is shown to have

been linked up with the moral and spiritual conduct of Man. The life of the last Prophet, peace be upon him, proves beyond all doubt that all authority ultimately belongs to Allah. He chooses those who obey Him and fight for His cause. When a nation disobeys Allah and upsets the code of life granted by Him then Allah sends warnings to that nation in the form of natural calamities. But if the nation does not repent and becomes more hard-hearted then He sends human beings to destroy those people. He also sows the seeds of discord among those nations which give up His code and proudly and arrogantly pose to be self-sufficient.[20]

This revealed form of historical discourse led Ashraf to argue that the Quran has divided Man's existence on the earth into three historical eras. The first historical era extends from the first prophet (Adam) to the last prophet of Islam (Muhammad). In this era, the history of Man seems to have been governed by a cyclic process, where the rise and fall of nations and races are revealed to be integrally related to their obedience or disobedience to the code of life given to them by God. The second era extends from the period of the Rightly Guided Caliphs to the regeneration of Man after the expected second coming of Jesus. The third era demonstrates man's gradual downfall until he loses all consciousness of values, and the whole human race and the creation will be destroyed by God.[21] This Quranic periodization of universal history revolves around the role of the Divine Laws of the universe and how they determine the rise and fall of civilizations, and contribute to continuity and change in world history. Our concern here is not to acknowledge the validity of this view or refute it, but rather to argue that it has motivated some Muslim historians to reject the current Western periodization scheme based on a threefold sequence—ancient, medieval and modern—which has been described by Croce as "an affair of imagination, of vocabulary, and of rhetoric, which in no way changes the substance of things."[22] It reflects the imagination and socio-cultural worldview of a very specific group of people at a very particular period of time. Consequently, there is no reason to periodize the history of Muslims and that of non-Western nations in accordance with this tripartite, ancient-medieval-modern scheme, because it is "a hallowed tradition" that resembles the German Romantic's view of the world and is "too parochial to be an adequate scheme of world history."[23]

Another work discussing the Quranic concept of history is that of Imad al-Din al-Khalil, entitled *Islamic Interpretation of History*. Khalil perceives the Holy Quran as a Divine Verdict on world history, where historians could find a number of laws that govern the rise and fall of nations and civilizations. This Quranic approach is shared by Khalid Blankinship, who acknowledges the validity of "the concept of *tawhid*" as the most important underlying principle that leads us to discern "the one unique thread that runs through all history, and not only the parochial history of the Muslims since the Prophet."[24] Here, the universality of *tawhid* emphasizes that the study of history should properly encompass the complete histories of all peoples since they contain the seeds of *tawhid*, and all human traditions contain elements that are more or less close to Islam, if Islam is the religion of all prophets.[25]

Based on this discussion, one may argue that these selected works have fairly influenced the structure and development of the programs offered by the Department of History and Civilization, and paved the way for their Islamization and integration with other revealed disciplines.[26] The subsequent paragraphs will address these issues with special focus on the structure and content of the undergraduate history and civilization program.

Structure of History and Civilization Program

The undergraduate history and civilization program is based on four components, namely, 1. the fundamental courses, 2. generic skills, 3. Islamic revealed knowledge and human science elective courses, and 4. history and civilization core courses.

The fundamental component contains the four introductory courses in communication, political science, psychology, and sociology and anthropology. The objective of this package is to equip students with an interdisciplinary approach that employs the methods and insights of other social disciplines in the study of history and civilization. This notion of a partnership between history and other social-science disciplines is not new. It can be traced back to the first two decades of the twentieth century, when the French historian and philosopher, Henri Berr (1863–1954 CE/1280–1374 AH), developed it into an interdisciplinary theory that appeals "for greater cooperation between social scientists and historians."[27] Berr's efforts eventually culminated in the establishment of the Annales

School of historiography in France in the late 1920s. The Annales School sprang from conviction that history should be "wide open to the findings and methods of other disciplines," and at the same time must resist the temptation to divide itself into a number of "specialisms" such as economic history and the history of ideas.[28]

The generic-skills component focuses on the language-proficiency and co-curricular activities. The language-proficiency courses are managed by the Centre for Languages and Pre-University Academic Development (CELPAD) and deal with English, Arabic and Malay languages. Proficiency in English is required because English is the primary medium of instruction, and working knowledge is required in Arabic language as the secondary medium of learning and in Bahasa Maleyu (for non-Malaysian students) for local communication. In addition to these language-proficiency courses, students are required to take co-curricular activity courses that handle spiritual, leadership and interest-based matters.

The third component is the six elective courses of Islamic revealed knowledge and two other courses from human sciences or other disciplines listed as minor. The primary aim of the Islamic revealed-knowledge package is to introduce students to Islamic concepts and views pertaining to the study of history and civilization through a survey of relevant passages from the Quran and Sunnah. This survey will familiarize students with the significance of the Quran and Sunnah as two important sources of Muslim history and civilization, and also encourage them to cultivate an Islamic perspective that will enhance their intellectual understanding of continuity and change in world history and civilizations.

The last and major component is the twenty-four core courses in history and civilization that focus on historical methods, theories, and subject matters. Three courses examine the development of historical methods and theories in Muslim and Western literatures. "HIST 1000: Introduction to History and Civilization" traces the development of historical criticism in classical Islamic literatures and highlights the contributions of Muslim scholars in the field of history and civilization. It also addresses various issues such as interpretation of history from Islamic and secular perspectives and factors behind rise and fall of civilizations. "HIST 2999: Research Methodology" concentrates on data collection, data analysis, writing techniques, social science research methods, and forms of historical writing. "HIST 3750:

Muslim Historiography" deals with the Quranic concept of history and traces the beginnings of historical criticism to the science of the *hadith* (prophetic tradition), where early Muslim historians utilized the methods and techniques of the *muhaddithun* (reporters) to test the authenticity of the sources and assess the accuracy of historical events. The course also outlines the development of historical criticism in Muslim historiography until the epoch of Ibn Khaldun (d. 1406 CE/808 AH), who was a highly vibrant and original thinker not only in the field of history, but in sociology and political science as well. These three courses aim at providing students with the historical methodology and rigorous scholarly attributes and prerequisite skills for interpretation of historical events, encouraging them to cultivate an Islamic perspective that will deal with world history in general and Muslim history in particular.

With this vision in mind, the Department of History and Civilization does not only concentrate on political history, but pays special attention to the study of culture and world civilizations.[29] Seven courses deal with the major civilizations of the world from the ancient Near Eastern civilizations to the contemporary Western civilization. The discussion on these civilizations is wrapped up in a 4000-level course entitled: "Rise and Fall of Civilizations." This course provides a critical survey of Muslim and Western interpretations of the rise and fall of civilizations, studies the distinctive features of major world civilizations such as Chinese, Indian, Muslim, and Western civilizations, highlights the underlying factors that determine the rise and fall of these civilizations, and emphasizes the importance of their co-existence and dialogue.

The remaining courses address world history from political, economic and cultural perspectives with emphasis on the history of the Muslim world from the time of the Prophet Muhammad to the abolition of the Ottoman caliphate in 1924 CE/1343 AH. They also examine the spread of Islam from its cradle in the Arabian Peninsula to the Maghrib and Spain, the Indian subcontinent, Sub-Saharan Africa, the Malay world, and Central and Southeast Europe. Other courses handle the modern and contemporary history of Southeast Asian countries and other Muslim nation-states during colonial and post-independence periods. For the modern history of the non-Muslim world, there are three courses that concentrate on the modern history of China and Japan, Europe, and the United States of America.

This survey may point out that the undergraduate history and civilization program does not cover the modern history of Central Asia, South America and Australia; and also pays modest attention to religious, economic, social, and women's history. However, the Department is aware of this limitation and is planning to introduce news courses that will address the above neglected areas. [30]

For graduation requirements, history and civilization students have four options: 1. Single Major, 2. Major with Minor, 3. Double Major, and 4. Double Degree. In the case of single majors, they are required to complete 72 credit hours of history and civilization core courses, 12 credit hours of introductory (fundamental) human sciences courses, 13 credit hours of generic skills courses, and 24 credit hours of Islamic revealed knowledge and human sciences elective courses (see Table 2). Those who intend to minor in a program in or outside the Kulliyyah are required to take 30 credit hours from the discipline concerned (see Table 3); and double majors must take 60 credit hours from the core component of the chosen human science program (see Table 4). Those who did their minor outside the Kalliyyah are entitled to do a double degree in another Kulliyyah on the condition that they fulfill the total graduation requirements of the program concerned (see Table 5).

Table 2. Single Major:
Bachelor of Human Sciences (History and Civilization).

No	Course content	Credit Hours	Number of courses
1.	Fundamental Content (introduction to human sciences)	12	4
2.	Generic Skills (Language and Co-curricular activities)	13	18
3.	History and civilization core courses	72	24
4.	Elective (6 Islamic Revealed Knowledge courses and 2 other courses from any department of IRKHS or other Kulliyyah which are listed as minor courses)	24	8
	Total	121	54

Table 3. Major with Minor:
Bachelor of Human Sciences (History and Civilization)
with Education (for example)[32]

No	Course content	Credit Hours	Number of courses
1.	Fundamental Content *(introduction to human sciences)*	12	4
2.	Generic Skills *(Language and Co-curricular activities)*	13	18
3.	History and civilization core courses	72	24
4.	Elective *(6 Islamic Revealed Knowledge courses and 2 other courses from any department of IRKHS or other Kulliyyah which are listed as minor courses)*	24	8
5.	Minor *(other human sciences progrmme, IRK, or other Kulliyyah)*	30	10
	Total	151	64

Table 4. Double Major:
Bachelor of Human Sciences (i.e. History & Civilization and Political Science)[33]

No	Course content	Credit Hours	Number of courses
1.	Fundamental Content *(introduction to human sciences)*	12	4
2.	Generic Skills *(Language and Co-curricular activities)*	13	18
3.	History and civilization core courses	72	24
4.	Elective *(6 Islamic Revealed Knowledge courses and 2 other courses from any department of IRKHS or other Kulliyyah which are listed as minor courses)*	24	8
5.	Major *(from the core component of another human Science Programme)*	60	20
	Total	181	74

Table 5. Double Degree:
Human Science Programme Double Degree with another Division/Kulliyyah[34]

No	Course content	Credit Hours	Number of courses
1.	Fundamental Content (*introduction to human sciences*)	12	4
2.	Generic Skills (*Language and Co-curricular activities*)	13	18
3.	History and civilization core courses	72	24
4.	Elective (*6 Islamic Revealed Knowledge courses and 2 other courses from any department of IRKHS or other Kulliyyah which are listed as minor courses*)	24	8
5.	Double Degree (*from another Division/Kulliyyah*)	120 or the total graduation requirements of the Kulliyyah concerned	40
	Total	241	94

Conclusion

This chapter supports the view of other social scientists who claim that the project for Islamization of knowledge has played an eminent role in contemporary scholarship and literature. This role manifested itself in a series of publications and in Islamized curricula and textbooks for undergraduate programs in various universities in the Muslim and non-Muslim worlds.[35] Nevertheless, these academic contributions do not deny that the Islamization project is at present facing a genuine challenge that emerges from three different academic arenas. Firstly, the absence of coherent epistemological and methodological bases upon which the Islamization of modern disciplines can flourish. Secondly, several Western-trained Muslim social scientists view with disfavor the Islamization of knowledge project and often have misconceptions of its aims, scope, processes, and procedures. Thirdly, the curricula of all human sciences at pre-university levels in the Muslim world are secular-oriented and need to be restructured in line with the vision of Islam. However, these challenges do not refute the validity of the Islamization of knowledge rationale that stems from the principle that the Western contemporary knowledge is often not in harmony with the Islamic fundamentals. But they alternatively generated two major approaches that address the Islamization of social sciences from distinct perspectives: "engagement" and "disengagement." The engagement group departs from the point that modern knowledge still has a valuable role in the Islamization process, while the disengagement group totally rejects the integration of Islamic and Western traditions of scholarship, and subscribes to the establishment of an Islamic methodology that will encourage the creativity of Muslim scholars within the revealed orbit of the Quran and the Sunnah. The engagement proponents pledge to the integration of knowledge derived from revealed and human sources, and favor the utilization of the methods and findings of the modern Western disciplines that are in harmony with the fundamentals of Islam for studying Muslim societies and heritage. To achieve this objective, they suggest the following procedural steps:[36]

1. Mastering modern social-scientific scholarship
2. Analysis of the historical development of the social sciences and identification of their ontological and epistemological underpinnings
3. Rigorous criticism of all of the above from Islamic perspectives
4. Integration with pertinent generated knowledge with reference to empirical reality

The academic staff of the Department of History and Civilization seems to have shared the standpoint of the engagement proponents and moved towards the setting up of a creative synthesis of the Islamic legacy and Western knowledge. This induces us to argue that the current practice of the Department of History and Civilization will contribute to the development of a pluralist approach to the teaching and learning of world history. Such an approach may release historians from the prevalent influence of the one-sided Western interpretation of history that denies the authority of revelation as a source of knowledge, and marginalizes the internal mechanisms governing the rise and fall of non-Western civilizations.

Notes

1. Ismail Raji al-Faruqi, *Islamization of Knowledge: The Problem, Principles and the Workplan*, (Herndon, VA, USA: International Institute of Islamic Thought, 1982). Al-Faruqi was born in 1921 CE/1340 AH in Yaffa, Palestine. He earned his B.A. in philosophy from the American University in Beirut, two master's degrees from Indiana and Harvard respectively, and a PhD in philosophy from Indiana University in 1952 CE/1372 AH. He later retreated to the quarters of al-Azhar in Cairo, Egypt, for three years to study Islam. He also held a teaching post at McGill University in Montreal, Canada. From there he moved to Pakistan, joining the Islamic Research Institute, which "gave him ample opportunity to apply his philosophy to religion or, more appropriately, to apply his religion to modern secular philosophy" and "to start on a course of an intellectual encounter with the West." In this academic environment, al-Faruqi laid down the foundation of his project on the Islamization of human knowledge. Nevertheless, his assassination in 1986 CE/1406 AH "dealt a severe blow to the Islamization movement making the process of awakening and recovery very difficult." For further detail see Abdul Rashid Moten, "Approach to Islamization of Knowledge: A Review," in Mohd. Yusof Hussain, ed. *Islamization of Human Sciences* (Kuala Lumpur: International Islamic University Malaysia, 2006), 50–52. *Islamization of Human Sciences* is a compilation of selected and edited papers that were presented at the International Conference on Islamization of Human Sciences organized by the Kulliyyah of Islamic Revealed Knowledge and Human Sciences, 4–6 August 2000 CE/3⁻5 Judah I 1421 AH.
2. *The Conference Book of the First World Conference on Muslim Education*, (Jeddah: King Abdul Aziz University, 1977).
3. Al-Faruqi, *Islamization of Knowledge*, 4–8.
4. Abdul Hamid AbuSulayman, *Crisis in the Muslim Mind* (Trans. Yusuf Talal DeLorenzo), 2nd ed. (Herndon, VA, USA: International Institute of Islamic Thought, 1987); AbuSulayman, *Islamization: Reforming Contemporary Knowledge*, (Herndon, Virginia, USA: International Institute of Islamic Thought, 1994), 2; al-Faruqi, *Islamization of Knowledge*, 6–8. AbuSulayman is a prominent co-founder of the Islamization of knowledge project, and a former and founding member of the International Institute of Islamic Thought, which was established in 1981. He was born in Makkah, Saudi Arabia, in 1936 CE/1355 AH. He earned his Bachelors in Commerce and Masters in Political Science from the University of Cairo. He received his PhD in international relations from the University of Pennsylvania, in 1973 CE/1393 AH. He held many administrative and teaching positions in his country and abroad, and he also served as the Rector of the International and Islamic University Malaysia from 1988 CE/1408 AH to 1998 CE/1418 AH. During his tenure the Centre of Fundamental Knowledge was promoted in the Faculty of Islamic Revealed and Human Sciences. See Moten, "Approach to Islamization," 58–59.
5. Abdul Hamid AbuSulayman, *Islamization: Reforming Contemporary Knowledge*, (Herndon, Virginia, USA: International Institute of Islamic Thought, 1994), 2.
6. Al-Faruqi, *Islamization of Knowledge*, 4; Abdul Hamid AbuSulayman, *Towards an Islamic Theory of International Relations: New Directions for Methodology and Thought*, (Herndon, VA, USA: International Institute of Islamic Thought, 1993), 4.
7. Al-Faruqi, *Islamization of Knowledge*, 9.
8. Ibid., 15.
9. Ibid., 22–38.

10. Ibid., 38–47.
11. Louay Safi, *The Foundation of Knowledge: A Comparative Study in Islamic and Western Methods of Inquiry*, (Kuala Lumpur: International Islamic University Malaysia Press, 1999), 8.
12. Rashid Moten, "Islamization of Knowledge: Why?" *Kulliyyah Research Bulletin*, 1, 1 (2006): 4. *International Islamic University Malaysia: Undergraduate Prospectus 1996* (Kuala Lumpur:
13. International Islamic University Malaysia, 1996), 1–2; *International Islamic University Malaysia: Undergraduate Prospectus 2004* (Kuala Lumpur: International Islamic University Malaysia, 2004).
14. Mohd Kamal Hassan, "Islamic Studies in Contemporary South East Asia: General Observations," in Islma-ae Alee et al., eds., *Islamic Studies in ASEAN: Presentations of an International Seminar* (Pattani Campus, Thailand: College of Islamic Studies, Prince Songkla University, 2000), 480.
    Mohd Kamal Hassan is the Founding Dean of the Kulliyyah of Islamic Revealed Knowledge and Human Sciences. He obtained his M.A. (1970 CE/1390 AH), M.Phil. (1973 CE/1393 AH), and PhD (1976 CE/1396 AH) from Columbia University. In 1982 CE/1403 AH, when the government of Malaysia decided to establish the International Islamic University, he was invited to assist in the planning of the project. He was instrumental in formulating the philosophy, vision, mission and objectives of the International Islamic University Malaysia. He held various senior administrative posts until 1997 CE/1418 AH, when he was appointed as a visiting professor and the first holder of the newly created Malaysian Chair of Islam in Southeast Asia at the Centre for Muslim-Christian Understanding, Georgetown University, Washington D.C., for a period of two years. Upon the completion of his mission, he was appointed as Rector of the IIUM until May 2006 CE/Rabi' I 1427 AH.
15. *Self-analysis Report*, Department of History and Civilization, IIUM, 2006.
16. Abdul Hameed Siddiqi, *The Islamic Concept of History* (Lahore: Kazi Publications, 1981).
17. Syed Ali Ashraf, *The Quranic Concept of History*, 2nd ed. (London: The Islamic Foundation, 1985).
18. Ibid., 8.
19. Ibid., 9.
20. Ibid.
21. Ibid., 11.
22. Benedetto Croce, *History: Its Theory and Practice*, 2nd ed, (New York, Russell and Russell, 1960), 110.
23. Khalid Blankinship, "Islam and World History: Towards a New Periodization,", *The American Journal of Islamic Social Science* 8 (1995): 423, 426. For further detail on periodization of world history see William A. Green, "Periodizing World History," in: Philip Pomper et al., eds., *World History: Ideologies, Structures and Identities* (Oxford: Blackwell Publishers, 1998), 53–65.
24. Khalid Blankinship, "Islam in World History," 441.
25. Ibid., 442.
26. For further detail see the papers presented at "Islamization of Knowledge in Studying History: A One-Day Symposium," Department of History and Civilization (IIUM), March 7, 1996 CE/ Shawal 16, 1416 AH.
27. Harry Ritter, *Dictionary of Concepts in History* (New York: Greenwood Press, 1986), 240–241
28. Ibid.

29. Hassan Ahmed Ibrahim, "The Study of History: Introductory Remarks," 4. (Paper presented at the "Islamication of Knowledge" symposium.) Hassan Ahmed Ibrahim obtained his PhD (1970 CE/1390 AH) in history from the School of Oriental and African Studies, University of London. He held various senior academic and administrative posts in his home country (Sudan) and abroad. He served as head of the Department of History and Civilization, IIUM, from 1996 to 2002 CE/1417 to 1423 AH, and he is currently the Deputy Dean for Postgraduate Studies and Research, IKRHS.
30. Mohsen M.S. Saleh, "Developing a History Curriculum: An Islamic Perspective," *Intellectual Discourse* 9 (2001): 95. Associate Professor Mohsen M. S. Saleh was the head of the Department of History and Civilization from 2002 to 2003 1423 to 1424 AH . He is currently the founding Director General of al-Zaytouna Centre for Consultation and Strategic Studies.
31. *New Programme Structure, Kulliyyah of Islamic Revealed Knowledge and Human Sciences, Human Sciences Division* (International Islamic University Malaysia, 2006), 2.
32. Ibid., 2.
33. Ibid., 5.
34. Ibid., 6.
35. Mohamed Aslam Haneef, *A Critical Survey of Islamization of Knowledge* (Kuala Lumpur: Research Centre, IIUM, 2005), 48–49. Haneef's critical survey gives a comprehensive review of Islamization of knowledge, discussing the views of its main proponents as well as its critics. It covers a series of issues pertaining to the definitions of Islamization of knowledge, its rationale and process. The book provides a very useful reference material for those who are interested in the Islamization of knowledge project and its development and challenges.
36. For further detail see Ibrahim A. Rajab, "The Methodology of Islamizing Human Sciences," in Hussain, *Islamization of Human Science*, 73–99; "On the Nature and Scope of the Islamization Process: Towards Conceptual Clarification," *Intellectual Discourse* 3 (1995): 113–122.

CHAPTER 4

Creating Global History from Asian Perspectives

Shigeru Akita

The purpose of this essay is to introduce a new attempt to create a Global History from Asian perspectives at my department of world history, in the graduate school of letters, Osaka University, and to induce many scholars to join in this challenging project.

The COE Joint Research Project—"Global History and Maritime Asia"
Some colleagues and I participated in the Twenty-first Century COE (Centre of Excellence) Program <Interface Humanities> in April 2004 and closely collaborated with the team of Shiro Momoki.[1] We formed a research group called "Global History and Maritime Asia" and continued to hold two sets of interrelated seminars and workshops on this research subject: a Global History Seminar and a Maritime Asia Seminar.

The aims of our project are twofold. Firstly, we are trying to overcome academic barriers among the three conventional divisions of departmental and research fields in Japanese historical studies, that is, Japanese history, oriental history and western history. Our graduate school has been a pioneer among Japanese national universities in creating the Department of World History by merging the Asian and Western History Departments in 1998. We have tried to create a new type of transnational or inter-regional history in the context of a global perspective. The second aim is to accelerate academic dialogue and discussion with foreign scholars in different fields of study, and to propagate the excellent works of Japanese scholars to the wider world. Japanese scholars used to publish their articles and books in Japanese, but due to language barriers and the lack of translation, dialogues between Japanese-medium historical studies and English-medium researches were difficult to manage. In order to fill this gap, our research group on global history has tried to organize almost all seminars and workshops in English.

We started our joint research activities on global history in September 2003 and have organized a series of seminars (twenty-four) and workshops (nine) as well as a December 2007 international conference, inviting prominent foreign and Japanese scholars.[2] Our efforts to organize seminars and workshops were supported financially by the Suntory Cultural Foundation (Osaka) in 2003–04 as well as by the Twenty-first Century COE Program <Interface Humanities> and the JFE Twenty-first Century Foundation (Tokyo) in 2007. We also received a grant-in-aid for scientific research from the Japan Society for the Promotion of Science (JSPS) for three years, 2005–2007.

Research Activities in Global History Seminars and Workshops

Global history—comparison and interconnectedness. Recently, "global history" is attracting much attention from many scholars in the world. We use the term "global history" to refer to a kind of transnational or mega-regional history in the context of the formation and development of a capitalist world-economy or the formation of the Modern World-System. It closely relates to the historical origins and the progress of globalization since the early modern times.

As a prominent scholar in global history, Patrick O'Brien, has pointed out, "comparisons and connections are the dominant styles of global history."[3] In other words, an important aspect of global history is the history of the formation of mutual interdependence or interconnectedness among the various regions or areas in the world under the framework of a capitalist world-economy. The progress of globalization has promoted the formation of interconnected economic linkages beyond national borders, at various levels of transnational movements, including exchanges of goods, peoples, money, technology and information. Through study of the process and the progress of globalization, we can better interpret modern world history not only from comparative perspectives, but also from the perspective of the formation of relational history within a capitalist world-economy.[4]

As the studies of the Wallersteinian school have pointed out, the progress of globalization or the formation of the Modern World-System was promoted and accelerated by the presence of three hegemonic states in a capitalist world-economy, that is, the primacy of the Netherlands in the seventeenth century, the hegemony of Great Britain in the nineteenth century (Pax Britannica), and the predominance of the United States in the twentieth century (Pax Americana).[5] A hegemonic state provides "public goods" for the international system as a whole. These international public goods include "peace, safe access to international waterways, international laws for the protection of property rights, an open regime for foreign trade, and an international monetary system."[6]

However, these orthodox interpretations of the Modern World-System are challenged by the emergence of new studies about the modern world-economy focused on Asia, and by the progress and recent developments of Asian economic history in Japan as well as in the Anglo-American academic world.[7] As I will explain later, the main focus of reconsideration and the front line of new researches are concerned with the early modern world (the long eighteenth century) and the rapid transformation of contemporary East Asia (the East Asian Miracle). Therefore, the major theme of our seminars and workshops is to reconsider the formation and development of the Modern World-System from Asian perspectives, focusing especially on the early modern world of the long eighteenth century and on the contemporary twentieth century.

Collaboration with the Global Economic History Network project. Our global history seminar has a special academic connection with the international joint research project of the Global Economic History Network (GEHN).[8] The GEHN project is internationally organized by four universities, each with a key organizer: London School of Economics (Patrick K. O'Brien), University of California – Irvine (Kenneth Pomeranz), University of Leiden (Peer Vries), and Osaka University (Kaoru Sugihara, now working at Kyoto University), and it was financially supported by the Leverhulme Trust in the UK. The GEHN group has organized ten workshops in three years from 2003. In Osaka, Sugihara and his colleague, Takeshi Abe, organized the fifth GEHN workshop on cotton textiles in the nineteenth and twentieth centuries, in December 2004. By utilizing the GEHN global network, we were able to invite the following prominent economic historians to Osaka: Jan Luiten van Zanden (Utrecht), David Washbrook (Oxford), Jack Goldstone (George Mason), Patrick O'Brien (LSE), Kent G. Deng (LSE), Gareth Austin (LSE), R. Bin Wong (University of California – Los Angeles), Kenneth.Pomeranz (Irvine), and B. R. Tomlinson (School of Oriental and African Studies) among others. The global history seminar is usually co-organized by the graduate school of letters as well as by the graduate school of economics, and we continue to take interdisciplinary approaches to this attractive new agenda.

The GEHN program has been divided into the following five themes of global economic history:

A. The Formation, Development and Operation of Regional, National and International Markets (Markets);
B. The Geopolitical and Imperial Contexts for Economic Activity (Imperialism and Geopolitics);
C. Religious Values, Ideologies, Family Systems, Promoting and Restraining Economic Growth (Cultures);
D. Regimes for the Production of Useful and Reliable Knowledge (Science and Technology);
E. Convergence and Divergence in Standards of Living (Real Wages).

At the Osaka seminars and workshops on global history, we mainly focused our arguments and discussions on themes A, B, and E, due to the availability of Japanese scholars and our accumulation of academic work and researches.

The arguments of the GEHN group were strongly influenced by the provocative books and interpretations on the China-centered early modern world-economy presented by the so-called "California School" in economic history, including such people as Kenneth Pomeranz, Bin Wong, Jack Goldstone and Dennis Flynn. In particular, Pomeranz's *The Great Divergence* shows us that as recently as 1750, parallel economic developments occurred in Northwest Europe and East Asia, and that Europe's nineteenth-century divergence from the Old World owes much to the two fortuitous factors of the location of coal and the resources of New World.[9] On the other hand, my former colleague at Osaka University, Kaoru Sugihara, independently proposed his original interpretation of the "East Asian Path of Economic Development."[10] These two new interpretations attracted much attention from various scholars not only in Japan and Asia but also in Europe and the U.S., and provoked debates on the "Great Divergence" thesis. Strongly influenced by these two leading arguments in the context of Asian economic history, we tended to focus on the reconsideration of the early modern history of East Asia and Europe, by using the concept of "the long eighteenth century."

International order of Asia and hegemonic states in the twentieth century. In addition to the reconsideration of the "Great Divergence" thesis in economic history, we also considered the subject of international order of Asia in the twentieth century, which is closely related to theme B of the GEHN project (Imperialism and Geopolitics).

As I mentioned earlier, the Modern World-System was sustained and stabilized by the presence of hegemonic states. Thus the rise and fall of hegemonic states and the transformation or the shift of hegemony became important subjects to explore in the field of global history. In this historical context, British imperial history can now be seen as a "bridge" to global history.[11] British imperial historians P. J. Cain and A. G. Hopkins suggest that imperialism and empires can be viewed as globalizing forces in their second edition of *British Imperialism 1688–2000*.[12] And Patrick O'Brien has observed about the nineteenth century as follows: "Trade promoted and was in turn sustained by movements of capital, migrations of labour and transfers of technology and information around the world on an unprecedented scale and at ever increasing speeds. Political impediments to international flows of exports, imports, money, credit capital, labour, technology and information diminished sharply during the liberal international order that prevailed between 1846 and 1914."[13] We have already evaluated the role played by Great Britain in a capitalist world-economy and its implications for international relations. Especially, we reconsidered the international order of East Asia in the first half of the twentieth century, which was partly shaped by Britain's influence but kept a relatively unique "autonomous" status in a capitalist world-economy.

However, in order to consider the historical origins of the contemporary "East Asian Miracle," it is indispensable to understand the formation and development of American hegemony (Pax Americana) and its implications for Asian international order. Therefore, we tried to explore the mutual interactions between the Cold War system in East Asia and the rapid economic development of the Pacific-rim countries of East Asia since the 1960s. This line of argument used to be confined to the fields of diplomatic history or studies of security issues. By inviting prominent scholars such as Bruce Cumings of the University of Chicago (Korean War studies), Ilya V. Gaiduk of the Russian Academy of Sciences (Cold War studies), and Zhu Yingquan of Nanjing University (international relations from a Chinese perspective), we explored the politico-economic linkages of mutual interdependence between American strategy and industrialization in East Asia.

Integration of area studies into global history. As Patrick Manning pointed out in his thoughtful book on the current historiography of "world history" in the United States, area-studies scholarship was to contribute to the revolution in historical studies, both by applying social-scientific research and by recognizing global patterns. "Within the area-studies framework, comparative analysis has been central in the methodology of transnational studies."[14] We have also tried to integrate excellent work in area studies, especially Asian studies, with which we are more familiar and where we have the comparative advantage of multi-archival researches in indigenous Asian languages. We have already examined interactions between South Asian studies, Northeast Asian studies, and global history through the seminars on South Asia (by David Washbrook, B. R. Tomlinson and Tsukasa Mizushima) and the workshops on Northeast Asia (by David Wolff, Robert Bickers, Jürgen Osterhammel, Yukimura Sakon, and Toru Kubo). The interactions between the universal and the local are explored as the main theme of global history by a joint research group at the University of Texas, Austin, led by A. G. Hopkins.[15] Since the late nineteenth century, the concept of "transfer" or "transplantation" of certain social values, thoughts, and cultures from the West to Asia and their transformation or adaptation by Asian countries have often been discussed in a traditional Japanese and Asian academic context of westernization or modernization. However, we put strong emphasis on mutual connections and relationships in both directions between Asia and the West (Europe and the United States).

In order to examine the interactions or connections between the regional factors revealed through area studies and global history, we organized three workshops on maritime history. The team of Shiro Momoki and Kayoko Fujita organized two international workshops with the Asian Research

Institute, National University of Singapore, led by Anthony Reid, entitled "Dynamic Rimlands and Open Heartlands: Maritime Asia as a Site of Interactions," in October 2004 in Naha (Okinawa) and in October 2006 in Nagasaki. We attempted to bring about constructive dialogues between (Japanese-medium) Northeast Asian maritime history and (English-medium) Southeast Asian maritime history. They are now editing two books based on the results of workshops, which will be published in English and Japanese. In addition to these two workshops from Asian perspectives, we held another workshop on "Maritime Trade and Trading Metropoles: Europe and Asia, 17th to 20th Centuries," in August 2006 in Hamburg, in collaboration with Universität Hamburg (Franklin Kopitzsch, Frank Hatje, Klaus Weber and Toshiaki Tamaki) and the Wirtschaftsgeschichtliche Forschungsstelle. At this German workshop, we tried to implement comparative studies of maritime history in the early modern European and Asian cases, by focusing on the roles of merchant networks and connections among imperial maritime ports.

Teaching World History

"World History Summer School" for senior high school teachers. In addition to the seminars and workshops on global history and maritime history of Asia, we are holding the "World-History Summer School" for senior high school teachers in mid-August as a part of the COE project. The aim of the summer school is to promote a dialogue between academic historians and high school teachers in the field of world history. The subject of world history had developed as an important course of study at Japanese senior-high schools after the Second World War, and became part of the compulsory curriculum in the early 1990s. It brought a great demand for and interest in academic discussions on the recent historiography and new interpretations of global history. Therefore, on a teaching level, we use two key-terms, "World History" and "Global History" compatibly for practical purposes, and recently started to use the term "Global World History."

My colleagues and I have already written several school textbooks and sub-texts at the request of two textbook companies, and attracted keen attention from senior high-school teachers.[16] In considering this popularity and a great social need for a dialogue among universities, high schools, text publishing companies and mass media, we started the "World-History Summer School" in 2003.

We have taken the following big topics for themes of discussion: the Silk Road and World History (2003), Japanese history in the context of Asian history (2004), New Historical Studies and Education of History (2005), and the Challenge of Historical Studies at Osaka University (2006). Fortunately, this summer school for "World History" became very popular among well prepared teachers, and we had around 400 participants from throughout the country in the past four years. It was also reported in several national newspapers and newsletters of teachers' associations.

In addition, from October 2005, we received support from another new fund of the Japanese Education Ministry in order to improve and develop graduate studies in world history for two years.[17] This fund, a national "Initiative for an Attractive Education in Graduate School" (IAE), granted aid in a nationwide competition, like the COE project, and around 50 programs were approved in fields including natural sciences, technology, and medical science. By utilizing this new fund, we started a monthly seminar on world history, inviting active senior high-school teachers who participated in our summer school.[18] The aims of this new seminar are twofold: continuing education of senior high-school teachers in world history, and wider training of our graduate students in transnational and trans-cultural studies. We usually arrange two reports on the common topic—one from an academic historian and the other from a school teacher—and try to link the two presentations together to create a new course in world history. From 2006, this seminar was formally recognized as a course for our graduate students and around ten students will attend. We have discussed the following topics: new developments in Southeast Asian history, recent historiography of Islamic studies, American empire, religious studies of modern times, world history and the collapse of socialism in Eastern Europe, and so on. Through an intimate dialogue at seminars, e-mail and website networks with high school teachers, and in national newspapers, we are applying the results of our research activities to the wider society, making a strong appeal to the public on the importance of historical studies.

Team teaching on "the frontier of historical studies." As a regular lecture course for graduate students at the master's level, we have a one-year team-teaching program on "the frontier of historical studies," including twelve scholars since 2003. This is an introduction to methodology and the new historiography of historical studies for master's-level students. This course is jointly taught with scholars from Osaka University of Foreign Studies (OUFS), which is specialized in area studies, especially in Asia-Pacific studies. Our team consists of seven scholars from Osaka University (European history, Japanese history, British imperial history, Southeast Asian history, Japanese studies, art history of East Asia and studies of comparative civilizations) and five from OUFS (modern Chinese studies, overseas Chinese studies, central-Eurasian studies, East European studies, and studies of comparative cultures). The basis of this course was formed and strengthened through the various collaborations of joint-research projects, including the COE and area-studies program of the past ten years.

Two months before the beginning of the course, we will have a half-day intensive discussion among our team and try to share common targets to coordinate each title of teaching. We usually set two common themes for teaching out of the following six: 1. the advantage of comparative history, 2. beyond national history and searching for regional history, 3. historical studies and the contemporary world, 4. the turning points in history, 5 historical theories and approaches, and 6. historical materials for research. The most important point of this team-teaching is to share the aims among scholars and to coordinate and adjust each title, by using e-mail network and the help of two teaching assistants. Fortunately, we usually have about twenty students from both universities for this course, and we are now editing a one-volume book for this course.[19] We also started, in 2005, a similar joint introductory class for undergraduate students in the Department of World History and the Department of Japanese History. These teaching classes illustrate the gradual development of the world history curriculum at Osaka University and the positive, cooperative relationships and networks developed with related scholars and universities.

Future Directions of Global History

From 2005, in order to expand further our research on global history, I started a new joint-research project on global history with six colleagues: Toru Kubo (Shinshu University: modern Chinese economic history), Tsukasa Mizushima (University of Tokyo: economic history of South Asia), Wolfgang Schwentker (Osaka University: comparative studies of civilizations), Kaoru Sugihara (Kyoto University: Asian economic history), Toshiaki Tamaki (Kyoto Sangyo University: maritime and international commercial history of early-modern Europe), and Norihisa Yamashita (Ritsumeikan University: studies of the Modern World-System). We received a grant-in-aid for scientific research from the JSPS for three years.

We are now holding a series of seminars and workshops and editing their proceedings. Schwentker presents us with the historiography of global history, mainly focusing on studies in a German-speaking academic world, with which he has an intimate collaborating relationship, especially through his strong connection with the so-called "Vienna School" of global history. Yamashita examines the World-System analysis from Asian perspectives and proposes an alternative analytical framework of the empires and "the long twentieth century."

In addition to these two theoretical analyses on global history, we are now trying to create two related sub-fields in global history, based on our own empirical case studies. The first is "global economic history—comparison and connection." Economic history is one of the most advanced sub-fields in global history. By utilizing the GEHN academic network, we are exploring global economic history. A comparison of mega-regions on a Eurasian continental scale, including Europe, South Asia, East Asia and Japan in the long eighteenth century, is a newly emerging subject for us. We also adopt a relational approach to reveal interconnectedness or linkages, as distinctive features of our project. Tamaki and Mizushima cover the long eighteenth century with reference to maritime history, and the arguments of Kubo and myself are related to the international economic order of East Asia in the twentieth century. The second sub-field is "global intellectual and institutional history—transfer and transplantation." This field addresses the "transfer" or "transplantation" of cultures, thoughts, and social value systems from the West to Asia and vice versa. In applying this approach, we may think of a global intellectual history and a global institutional history. For this purpose, we have already had a workshop with a German scholar, Jürgen Osterhammel (Konstanz) in January 2006.

Our efforts to create global history from Asian perspectives started only four years ago. We would like to expand our seminars and workshops in Osaka by inviting more foreign and Japanese scholars in this developing field. We are planning to organize a three-day international workshop on "Interactions of Commodities and Information in Global History: Seventeenth to Twenty-first Centuries" in December 2007.

Notes

1. www.let.osaka-u.ac.jp/coe/interface_php/english/index/index_e.html.
2. See the list of seminars and workshops on our website: www.let.osaka-u.ac.jp/seiyousi/info-2-grobal-1en.html.
3. Patrick K. O'Brien, "The State, Status and Future of Universal History," an essay submitted for Major Theme 1A, "Perspective on Global History, Concepts and Methodology" for the Nineteenth International Congress of Historical Sciences, Oslo, 6–13 August 2000, p.16; Patrick O'Brien, "Historiographical Traditions and Modern Imperatives for the Restoration of Global History," *Journal of Global History* 1 (2006): 4–7. Patrick O'Brien is Centennial Professor at the London School of Economics, and the Convenor of the Global Economic History Network (GEHN).
4. Minoru Kawakita, "Kindai-Sekai Sisutemu-ron wo megutte" [On the Modern World-System], *Senshu-Daigaku Shakai-Kagaku Kenkyusho Geppou* [*Monthly Report of the Institute of Social Sciences, Senshu University*, Tokyo], No.287 (1987).
5. Giovanni Arrighi, *The Long Twentieth Century: Money, Power, and the Origins of Our Times* (London and New York: Verso, 1994); Takeshi Matsuda and Shigeru Akita, eds., *Hegemoni-Kokka to Sekai Sisutemu* [*The Hegemonic States and the World System*] (Tokyo: Yamakawa-Shuppan, 2002).
6. Patrick K. O'Brien, "The Pax Britannica and the International Order 1688–1914," in Shigeru Akita and Takeshi Matsuda, eds., *Looking Back at the 20th Century: The Role of Hegemonic State and the Transformation of the Modern World-System*, (Proceedings of the Global History Workshop Osaka, 1999, Osaka University of Foreign Studies, 2000), 44–45.
7. R. Bin Wong, *China Transformed: Historical Change and the Limits of European Experience* (Ithaca: Cornell University Press, 1997); Takeshi Hamashita, *Choukou Shisutemu to Kindai-Ajia* [*Tributary System and Modern Asia*] (Tokyo: Iwanami publisher, 1997); A. G. Frank, *ReOrient: Global Economy in the Asian Age* (Berkeley and London: University of California Press, 1998); Kenneth Pomeranz, *The Great Divergence: China, Europe, and the Making of the Modern World Economy* (Princeton: Princeton University Press, 2000).
8. www.lse.ac.uk/collections/economicHistory/GEHN/Default.htm.
9. Pomeranz, *The Great Divergence*.
10. Kaoru Sugihara, "The East Asian Path of Economic Development: A Long-term Perspective," Discussion Papers in Economics and Business 00–17 (October 2000, Graduate School of Economics and Osaka School of International Public Policy (OSIPP), Osaka University). Later included in Giovanni Arrighi, Takeshi Hamashita and Mark Selden, eds., *The Resurgence of East Asia: 500, 150 and 50 year Perspectives*, (London and New York: Routledge, 2003), 78–121.
11. Shigeru Akita, ed., *Gentlemanly Capitalism, Imperialism and Global History* (Basingstoke and New York: Palgrave-Macmillan, 2002), 1–16.
12. P .J. Cain and A. G. Hopkins, *British Imperialism, 1688–2000*, 2nd ed. (Harlow and New York: Longman, 2001).
13. O'Brien, "The State Status and Future of Universal History," 8.
14. Patrick Manning, *Navigating World History: Historians Create a Global Past* (New York and Basingstoke: Palgrave Macmillan, 2003), 145–148.
15. A. G. Hopkins, ed., *Global History: Interactions between the Universal and the Local* (Basingstoke and New York: Palgrave Macmillan, 2006).

16. For example, Minoru Kawakita, Shiro Momoki et al., eds., *Koutou Sekaishi B* [*World History*] (Tokyo: Teikoku-shoin, 2003); Hiroshi Mukaiyama, Shigeru Akita et al., eds., *Sekaishi A* [*World History*] (Hiroshima: Daiichi Gakushusha, revised edition, 2006); Minoru Kawakita and Shiro Momoki, eds., *Tapestry*, 3rd ed. (Tokyo: Teikoku-shoin, 2006).
17. www.let.osaka-u.ac.jp/initiative/index.html/index.html (in Japanese).
18. www.geocities.jp/rekikyo/ (in Japanese).
19. Shigeru Akita and Shiro Momoki, eds., *Kokka to Chiki* [*States and Regions: the Frontier of Historical Studies*] (Osaka: Osaka University Press, forthcoming, 2008).

CHAPTER 5

Teaching Modern Global History at Nankai: A Noncentric and Holistic Approach

Zhang Weiwei

For many years, I have been trying to teach modern global history from a noncentric approach at Nankai University, Tianjin, China. Why do I try to do this? This is a question I have often asked myself. Another question that always haunts me is, how can I do this? It seems more difficult to find an answer for the latter.

As a student of world history, I was taught and trained essentially in Eurocentric scholarship from Karl Marx and Frederick Engels to Max Weber, Arnold J. Toynbee, Fernand Braudel, William H. McNeill, L. S. Stavrianos, Immanuel Wallerstein, E. L. Jones, and many other Western historians and theorists. In the circumstances of China, I was first influenced by the world history textbooks written by Soviet historians and then have been mostly influenced by those written by Western scholars. I have recommended Stavrianos's *The World Since 1500: A Global History* and Wallerstein's *The Modern World-System* to my students for reference.[1] But the more I taught "world history" in a Eurocentric approach, the more I found that something must be wrong in world-history theories and practices. I began to wonder whether the picture of world history in my mind and the one I showed my students at Nankai was a real and whole one. I found out that the "world history" in my mind was too Eurocentric and that the rest of the world had been either ignored or marginalized. Another reason for me to turn to a noncentric and holistic global history[2] was that "world history" and Chinese history are two separate disciplines in China, so that Chinese history is rarely studied in the context of global history and the received or dominant understanding of Chinese history in global history has been based on centrism and is misleading. I think "world history" or global history, as I prefer, needs to be rethought and re-envisioned from an alternative perspective.

In rethinking global history, I was inspired by Chuang Tsu and F. Engels. Chuang Tsu presents the dialogue of Shade and Shadow.

> Shade said to Shadow, "A little while ago, you were moving; and now you are standing still. A little while ago, you were sitting down; and now you are getting up. Why all this indecision?" Shadow replied, "Don't I have to depend on others to be what I am? Don't others also have to depend on something else to be what they are? My dependence is like that of the snake on his skin or of the cicada on his wings. How can I tell why I do this, or why I do that?"[3]

Engels, in an 1890 letter, pointed out that, "History is made in such a way that the final result always arises from conflicts between many individual wills, of which each again has been made what it is by a host of particular conditions of life. Thus there are innumerable intersecting forces, an infinite series of parallelograms of forces which give rise to one resultant—the historical event. This may again itself be viewed as the product of a power which works as a whole, unconsciously and without volition. For what each individual wills is obstructed by everyone else, and what emerges is something that no one willed. Thus past history proceeds in the manner of a natural process and is essentially subject to the same laws of motion."[4]

It seems to me that the two thinkers share the same idea of interdependence or contingency although they were very far apart in terms of times and places. Gradually, I figured out that global history is a noncentric and holistic evolution of humanity—diversity in unity. My understanding of global history can be summarized in the following points:

1. The single unit of analysis is the globe and the history of humanity as a whole in space and time to the extent that we can know it.
2. It is global disequilibrium[5] that has determined global history in general and shaped the histories of the incomparable parts (nation-states in particular). Global disequilibrium is absolute. Global equilibrium is relative.

3. Global disequilibrium was precipitated by the internal contradictions of a resultant in global history, that is, the combination of ecological, economical, political, military, social, cultural, religious, psychological and other forces, no matter whether they functioned or not.
4. From a holistic perspective, there has been a mix in terms of relations of production and social relations in global history.

So, in my classes, I try to prove that developments of civilizations in Eurasia, Africa, the Americas, Australia, and Oceania have been interdependent more or less and that a part (nation-state) has to depend on others to develop. For example, the historical changes of Spain in the fifteenth and sixteenth centuries had to depend on what had happened in Eurasia and the Americas in terms of balance of power, science, technology, religions, and so on. Old civilizations like Egypt, India, and China are no exception. Nor are those "new" states in the Americas, Africa, Australia, Europe, and Asia.

One of the reasons for me to emphasize global history as a whole is that some of my students are undergraduates majoring in either World History (over 30 students) or Chinese History (over 40 students), who take the required course as part of General World History—divided into four parts: ancient, medieval, modern, and contemporary periods—in order to have a general idea of World History and a background for their further study. Others are graduates majoring in either World History (over 30, doing MA study in national or regional history and/or area studies such as European Studies, North American Studies, Latin American Studies, or Chinese History (over 50) in different periods of time. They take the required course of Professional English in History in order to have a better understanding of Western scholarship. Among them, about 10 graduates take an elective Seminar in World System, in which I try to let them know how differently global history has been painted so that they have a whole picture of it.

To help my students understand global history as a whole, I often refer to what I call my "egg theory." Mao Zedong offered us his famous example of egg and stone:

> Does materialist dialectics exclude external causes? Not at all. It holds that external causes are the condition of change and internal causes are the basis of change, and that external

causes become operative through internal causes. In a
suitable temperature an egg changes into a chicken, but no
temperature can change a stone into a chicken, because each
has a different basis.[6]

My argument here is that temperature can change an egg into a chicken, but it can also change an egg into a boiled one, a frozen one, or a rotten one, or whatever you want it to be. What makes the temperature different?

The holistic approach takes the globe as the single unit of analysis in global history. Global history is all within one eggshell just like "the universe in a nutshell."[7] From this perspective, all "foreign" affairs and "international" relations should be viewed as internal interactions and conflicts among parts of the whole in the context of global history. Mao Zedong pointed out, "The fundamental cause of the development of a thing is not external but internal; it lies in the contradictoriness within the thing."[8] Ranajit Guha pointed out, "If *limit*, as defined by Aristotle, is 'the first thing outside which there is nothing to be found and the first thing inside which everything is to be found,' , , , we shall try and think World-history in terms of what is unthinkable within its boundaries."[9] Although Hegel overstressed his "spiritual principle," he did agree to view world history "with a universal thought which runs throughout the whole."[10] A. G. Frank argues, "The point is, however, that the real question is not about any 'given society,' but about the world economy and global system as a whole, and that everything is 'internal' to that."[11] Of course, I'm not going to ban analyzing "internal" or "external" factors in the case of studying a national/regional history. What I want to make clear is that every factor is "internal" in the case of studying global history. So, it is only from the perspective of "internal" interdependence and interaction that the whys of a partial development (by which I mean development of a part in the whole) can be understood properly.

Then comes the concept of global disequilibrium. According to the *I Ching* (*Book of Changes*), *yin* and *yang* can be anything opposite to each other in nature, and it is the combination and interaction of *yin* and *yang* that cause change in everything.[12] This is Hegel's "union of the two extremes."[13] Mao Zedong wrote, "The law of contradiction in things, that is, the law of the unity of opposites, is the basic law of materialist dialectics."[14] Unlike the old proverb that East and West never meet, the East and the West did meet and interact in global disequilibrium in the case of global history. Extremes not only meet, they also coexist, interconnect, interact, and complement each other. The East, the West, the North, and the South are all parts of the global equilibrium and disequilibrium. They have functioned differently according to the division of labor and cooperation in global history.

The noncentric and holistic approach argues that global history has been determined by an all-inclusive global disequilibrium. Global disequilibrium is a disorder caused by the resultant of all forces (ecological, economical, political, military, social, cultural, religious, psychological, etc.) in global history. In other words, the global disequilibrium is a global crisis. The Chinese translation of "crisis" is two characters. One means "chaos" and the other "chance," indicating that chaos provides a chance. It is global disequilibrium that has forced development and shaped global history. For instance, the Pax Mongolica, the westward expansion of the Islamic Ottoman Empire, Europe's trade imbalance with the East, socioeconomic problems caused by natural and man-made disasters (the Black Death, wars, religious conflicts, etc.), as well as the psychological temptation of the Orient occasioned by Marco Polo's book in Europe. These and many other changes combined to create a global resultant that led to the global disequilibrium: a combination of mutual attraction and exclusion (racial, cultural, religious, economic, political, military, etc.) among various civilizations due to the struggle for survival. Several poor and small western European countries—Spain, Portugal, the Netherlands, and England in particular—had to go to sea for a living in order to survive. The result was worldwide exploration as well as the domino effect afterward.

Global history itself created the resultant, the "internal contradictions" and interactions based on all changing and unchanging forces, for its development. In my classes, I try to prove that all great historical events were nothing but the results of global disequilibrium, which created the necessity to change directly or indirectly: the rise and fall of empires/civilizations/nation-states, the Crusades, the "discovery" and explorations of the "New World," the Enlightenment, the Industrial Revolution, the birth of the United States of America, the world wars, the Cold War, the Terrorist attacks on September 11, 2001, and the war in Iraq in 2003. In other words, global history created itself as well as its parts. No matter how strong, any power/force (empire, kingdom, or nation-state), group, institution, figure and force (economic, political, military, cultural, religious) is only a part of global disequilibrium, created and manipulated by the historical resultant. No change can be possible without global disequilibrium. This perspective renders senseless and unreasonable the theory of hegemony—that is, the notion that the hegemonic center of the world moves from one place (country) to another over time. For example, empires (Roman, Han, Mongol, Spanish, British, etc.) were all created by global disequilibrium, which forced a part of the globe to function in a certain way in order to maintain the global equilibrium, not the other way around. In global disequilibrium, each part only functions as "the unconscious tool of history" positively or passively.[15] In global history, a part (nation-state or anything) was not what it wanted to be but what it had to be in global disequilibrium. This is interdependence, i.e. "I have to depend on others to be what I am."[16] This is why the holistic approach provides new explanations of the changing places and functions of a given nation-state in global history.

In the changing global disequilibrium, advantages become disadvantages and *vice versa*. And there is a rule of "the latecomer's advantage"—the latecomer has the advantage of learning from predecessors and then surpassing them while the "advanced" forerunner might be limited by its "advanced" advantages and might become relatively "backward" for lack of the need of changes or from difficulties in making changes. Because of global disequilibrium, the "backward" parts had to destroy their "backward" relations or to be destroyed. This explains why, in global history, it was often not the advanced parts but rather one or several (not all) "backward" parts that first achieved a "more advanced" level of production and social relations.

It seems difficult to answer David D. Buck's question: "Was It Pluck or Luck That Made the West Grow Rich?"[17] This is a question my students often ask. One answer may be both at the same time, based on what the West did in global history and depending on whether the global disequilibrium was in favor or not in favor of them. To me, the answer could also be neither pluck nor luck because the West only did what it had to do to survive in the state of global disequilibrium, nothing more!

For example, England, a part of an island, was not good at either agriculture or industry and lost most of her lands on the continent in the Middle Ages. Fortunately, the English were good at raising sheep, which led to enclosure and changes in social structure. England first had to export raw wool and then cloth to European markets and to develop overseas trade with Asia, and later with the Americas, Africa, and Australia. In global competition, the English had learned that, "The ordinary means therefore to encrease our wealth and treasure is by *Forraign Trade*, wherein wee must ever observe this rule; to sell more to strangers yearly than wee consume of their in value."[18] Since England had little to sell on the global market, the English had to sell others' productions as global middlemen—linking continents, making profits from buying and reselling manufactures and raw materials from or to Asia, the Americas, Europe, Australia, and Africa (including slaves). Sociopolitical changes and the mercantilist policy did help England in participating actively in the global market through trade and war. The British Empire offered the English/British a broader market that needed to be supplied and put great pressure on them to produce something more to sell, so as to meet the deficit caused by their long-standing unfavorable balance of trade. Markets in English colonies in America, Asia, Africa, and Australia and her unfavorable balance of trade led to the question: How could England sell more or, at least, buy less? So, producing some import substitutes, for instance, cotton textiles, might be a sound alternative. England was also pushed by her mercantilist policies to produce more to export into the American colonial market and Africa (for slaves) in order to keep up the profitable triangular and multiangular trades with Europe, the Americas, Africa, and Asia. While the Indians and the Chinese did not need to have their advanced cotton industries "mechanized," the English did need to mechanize their new cotton industry to cope with the competition from oriental imports and to meet, at least, the great domestic and colonial demands at that time. To England, it really was a question of "to be, or not to be."

The English/Europeans had been busy in the global market long before they "discovered" the Americas. So the opinion of Marx and Engels that, "modern industry has established the world market, for which the discovery of America paved the way,"[19] indeed raises a question similar to, "which comes first: chicken or egg?" Which came first: the global market or the so-called "Industrial Revolution"? It is beyond all doubt that there had been a global market long, long before the Industrial Revolution in its received definition. The Silk Roads (a nice but misleading name) had linked the two tips of Afro-Eurasia and established interaction all along those roads. Exploration further enlarged the global market. It was the necessity of the global market in the global disequilibrium that gave occasion to the "Industrial Revolution," though modern industry is only a result and a part of an ever-increasing global market.

I would suggest that the Industrial Revolution was only the logical result of a global disequilibrium caused by a global imbalance between supply and demand as well as a changing balance of power. Adam Smith pointed out rightly in the eighteenth century:

> The establishment of the European colonies in America and the West Indies arose from no necessity: and though the utility which has resulted from them has been very great, it is not altogether so clear and evident. It was not understood at their first establishment, and was not the motive either of that establishment or of the discoveries which gave occasion to it; and the nature, extent, and limits of that utility are not, perhaps, well understood at this day.[20]

So also were explorers like Columbus and inventors like James Watt driven by their individual motives and not fully cognizant of what they had done or their implications for global history. For instance, the cotton gin, invented by Eli Whitney in 1793 in the United States, not only helped provide England's cotton mills with cheap raw material but also made cotton "king" in the South and contributed to the prosperity of the slavery plantation system in the United States. As Engels pointed out, "The conquest of India by the Portuguese, Dutch and English between 1500 and 1800 had *imports from* India as its object—nobody dreamt of exporting anything there. And yet what a colossal reaction these discoveries and conquests, solely conditioned by the interests of trade, had upon industry: it was only the need for *exports to* these countries that created and developed large-scale industry."[21]

In reality, the "capitalist" modern industry in England was based not only on the "capitalist mode of production" in some areas at home but also on slave labor in the South of the United States, the feudalism of Europe, and those modes of production in Asia and Africa, in short, a mixed global economy. I think that, if there is a "capitalist" mode of production, it was not "born in Europe in the sixteenth century," but born in the global economy as part of a mixed mode of production of the globe. This is why I agree with Frank that we should "dare to abandon (the sacrosanct belief in) capitalism as a distinct mode of production and separate system"[22] and that "it is much better to cut (out) the Gordian knot of 'capitalism' altogether."[23]

Robert B. Marks is correct in saying that "the Industrial Revolution was historically contingent on global forces."[24] The Industrial Revolution was a historical necessity spawned from a global disequilibrium. But he overlooks England's positive functions in the global disequilibrium. "English pluck, inventiveness, or politics" did contribute a great deal to the global development and should be taken into account. The English had to be plucky and inventive and had to have a political system that favored global economic development in order to survive in the midst of global competition. In other words, the global disequilibrium found the fittest way to solve the global imbalance of demand and supply in England (or in just a part of it). What we have to keep in mind is that what happened in England was only the logical result of the mixed mode of production of the globe and was due to global disequilibrium. So, what the English/British did at that time should be neither overlooked nor overstated.

The received opinion that "Britain remained the unchallenged 'workshop of the world' during the century between 1770 and 1870"[25] has been challenged by Frank: "Britain was the 'workshop of/for the world'. NOT SO: Britain had a structural and merchandise trade deficit in EVERY year, which rose from 10 million pounds sterling in 1816 to 160 million in 1913. That is, in no year during that century was Britain even able or required to export as much merchandise, primarily manufactures except for coal, as it imported."[26]

This argument is basically an issue of how to estimate the place of a nation-state in the global economy. Thinking of the recent debates on whether China is going to be a "workshop of the world" in the twenty-first century and also on the trade deficits of many "developed" countries, it is really hard to offer a correct assessment without a holistic global perspective. The world economy is a holistic system in which each part (nation-state) functions differently according to the existing division of labor in global disequilibrium. Interdependence and interaction are the basic relations among different parts that function as both giver and taker in unequal bilateral or multilateral exchange relations. What are the implications of the British "structural and permanent merchandise trade deficit" for the global economy? To me, it seems that the British trade deficit meant trade opportunities and a favorable balance of trade for other countries in particular and the development of a global socioeconomy in general.

Thus Kenneth Pomeranz's concept of "the great divergence" actually deals with a great mix or a "great convergence" in global disequilibrium.[27] During the period from 1400 to 1900, the essence of global history was not a "great divergence" in national/regional perspective but, from a holistic perspective, a great convergence in terms of global socioeconomic development as well as interdependence and interactions among different parts of the globe.

I have tried to provide my students with another perspective to encourage them to think and discuss so that they could develop their own ideas and perspectives on global history. It works on some of them; of course, not all of them. Their responses are positive. After the courses, some of them do think of world/global history as useful background and a few find it interesting in itself as a specialization.

Notes

1. Leften Stavrianos, *The World Since 1500: A Global History*, 6th ed. (Englewood Cliffs, NJ: Prentice-Hall, 1991); Immanuel Wallerstein, *The Modern World-System: Capitalist Agriculture and the Origins of the European World-economy in the Sixteenth Century* (New York: Academic Press, 1974).
2. One of the reasons that I prefer the term "global history" to "world history" is that the word "world" has been used too frequently to mean something other than "global" or the "whole world," for instance, in the cases of "the Old World," "the New World," "world systems," "European world-system," etc.
3. Chuang Tsu, *Inner Chapters*, trans. Gia-Fu Feng and Jane English (New York: Knopf, 1974), 48.
4. Frederick Engels, "To J. Bloch, London, September 21–22, 1890," Karl Marx and Frederick Engels, *Selected Works in Two Volumes* (Moscow: Foreign Languages Publishing House, 1958), II:489.
5. Unlike the general equilibrium and disequilibrium in microeconomics, global disequilibrium and global equilibrium are not economic but all-inclusive.
6. Mao Tse-Tung, "On Contradiction," in *Selected Works of Mao Tse-Tung* (Peking: Foreign Languages Press, 1967), I:314.
7. Stephen Hawking, *The Universe in a Nutshell* (New York: Bantam Books, 2001), 200.
8. Mao Tse-Tung, "On Contradiction," 313.
9. Ranajit Guha, *History at the Limit of World-History* (New York: Columbia University Press, 2002), 7–8, quoting Aristotle, *Metaphysics: Books* Γ, Δ, E. trans. Christopher Kirwan (Oxford: Clarendon. 1971), Δ 17, p. 54.
10. G. W. F. Hegel, *Lectures on the Philosophy of World History*, trans H. B. Nisbet (New York: Cambridge University Press, 1975), 30.
11. Andre Gunder Frank, *ReORIENT: Global Economy in the Asian Age* (London: University of California Press, 1998), 42–43.

12. See *I Ching (Book of Changes)*, trans. James Legge (New York: Causeway Books, 1973).
13. Hegel, *Lectures*. 81.
14. Mao Tse-Tung, "On Contradiction," 311.
15. Karl Marx, "The British Rule in India," in Karl Marx and Frederick Engels, *Collected Works* (New York: International Publishers, 1979), 12:132.
16. Chuang Tsu, *Inner Chapters*, 48.
17. See David D. Buck's review article, "Was It Pluck or Luck That Made the West Grow Rich?" *Journal of World History* 10 (1999): 413–430.
18. Thomas Mun, *England's Treasure by Forraign Trade* (New York, 1910—first published London, 1664), 7.
19. Karl Marx and Frederick Engels, "Manifesto of the Communist Party," in Marx and Engels, *Collected Works* (New York: International Publishers, 1976), 6:486.
20. Adam Smith, *The Wealth of Nations* (New York, 1937—first published London, 1776), 525.
21. Engels, "To C. Schmidt, London, October 27, 1890," in Marx and Engels, *Selected Works in Two Volumes*, II:491.
22. A. G. Frank, "Transitional Ideological Modes: Feudalism, Capitalism, Socialism," in A. G. Frank and B. K. Gills. eds., *The World System: Five Hundred Years or Five Thousand?* (London and New York: Routledge, 1993), 214.
23. Frank, *ReORIENT*, 332.
24. Robert B. Marks, The Origins of the Modern World: A Global and Ecological Narrative (Lanham, MD: Rowman and Littlefield, 2002), 15.
25. L. S. Stavrianos, *Global Rift: The Third World Comes of Age*. (New York: 1981), 169.
26. Andre Gunder Frank, "LOCATION, LOCATION, LOCATION TO DISSIPATE AND ABSORB ENTROPY in the Nineteenth Century World Economy," Paper presented at International Studies Association Annual Meeting (Chicago Feb. 20–24, 2001), p. 8.
27. Kenneth Pomeranz, *The Great Divergence: Europe, China, and the Making of the Modern World Economy* (Princeton, NJ: Princeton University Press,:2000).

CHAPTER 6

World History and Global Studies at the University of Leipzig

Matthias Middell and Katja Naumann

The University of Leipzig has a long tradition of transnational and global perspectives on the past, in both teaching and research. Along with this tradition has gone an unusual degree of institutionalization reaching back in time as far as the seventeenth century, when Johann Burkhard Mencke was appointed chair in universal history. In precisely this period, history as a field of study was at a turning point from a "Historia Sacra" to a more secularized concept, following the ideas of the Enlightenment. Mencke clearly represented this kind of early modern historiography. His interest in a broad historical understanding, together with the support of the university, is only one expression of how the discovery of a whole new world outside of Europe, mirrored in the philosophies of the Enlightenment, was taken up by historians and integrated into academic structures. The recent history of studying and writing world history in Leipzig, however, might be more interesting and significant for embedding current efforts in their wider context.

In 1891 Karl Lamprecht became professor in Leipzig and immediately introduced new directions in conceptualizing historical thinking. Firstly, he pleaded for an enlargement of research perspectives to socio-economic developments of smaller regions and to an interest in broad historical entities and contexts. Secondly, he developed an emphasis in historical mentalities. And thirdly, he began to work on what would today be called transnational history, starting with his habilitation thesis on German and

French entanglements in economic and cultural affairs since the late Middle Ages. Although his approaches were heavily criticized by the majority—one might fairly say the mainstream—of his German colleagues,[1] he was able to establish the "Institut für Kultur- und Universalgeschichte" (Institute for Cultural and Universal History) in 1909 as a second institution within the university, next to the History Department, that dealt with historical questions. This institute became the first place within the German academic system where research and teaching of comparative and world history was institutionalized beyond the level of single chairs and individual professors.[2] It immediately stimulated parallel efforts, but Leipzig remained for a very long time the only place in Germany where world history was not only an intellectual horizon but also the topic of a structured teaching program.[3] Lamprecht's institute was particularly famous for its library, with historical writings covering all regions of the world, and for its practice of guest lectures, which brought scholars from Japan, China, the U.S., and various European countries to Leipzig. The intellectual stimulus that arose around the institute, with its rich resources for research, influenced intellectuals as different as Marc Bloch from France, Nicolai Iorga from Romania, Henri Pirenne from Belgium, and Cai Yanpei from China.[4]

At Lamprecht's death in 1915 the double structure of a concentration on national history in the History Department and a focus on comparative, transnational, or universal approaches at the "Institut für Kultur- und Universalgeschichte" had become well established: each of the structures attracted around 300 students per year. An attempt to close the institute developed but failed, and thus the project of implementing world history in teaching and in historiographical study could continue—ironically under one of the former critics of Lamprecht, Walter Goetz, who was appointed to Lamprecht's chair and who started in 1928 to edit the popular "Propyläen Weltgeschichte" (Propyläen World History).[5]

The tradition in world history was further strengthened by the next director of the institute, the sociologist Hans Freyer. It is well-known, of course, that Freyer's appointment was a result of his close relationship to the National Socialist regime in the 1930s, but then he was never member of the Nazi Party. And he was far away from Leipzig and Germany from 1938 to 1945, while leading the "German Institute" in Budapest. Furthermore, when he published his "World History of Europe" in 1948, nothing of any former idea of German or European superiority was left. On the contrary, Freyer declared Europe's dominance over the rest of the world to have been definitively overcome by new powers and a new world order which had, in his opinion, to be taken as the starting point for world historical analyses.[6] Nevertheless his work from the early 1930s, in which he argued for a "revolution from the right," provided sufficient ground for heavy attacks and accusations after 1945, when the universities in the Soviet zone were undergoing a drastic change of personnel implemented by the communist government. When Freyer left Leipzig to go to Münster, where his works on "industrial society" became influential, the institute was confronted once again with an uncertain future.

With the employment of Walter Markov in 1948, however, a continuous development of more than four decades began. Markov had been an assistant professor at the University of Bonn but his open resistance to the Third Reich (from 1935 he spent ten years in prison) did not provide him with a warm welcome on his return to Bonn. In Leipzig, on the other hand, from his appointment in the late 1940s to his retirement as director of the institute in 1974, he was to become a widely recognized specialist in international and comparative history as well as an innovative practitioner of a "history from below," that was inspired by Marxist thoughts and theory. He was accepted and honored not only within Germany and the Eastern bloc, but also in the Western world. During his career, which was interrupted a few times through conflicts with the communist party, (including his suspension from the party in 1951), he was a leading figure in the East German academic landscape. He supervised more than 200 dissertations and coordinated the re-establishment of area studies (African and Arab Studies as well as Eastern European History) at Leipzig. Under his guidance, the tradition of comparative history was carried into the 1950s and 1960s and was enriched by a close cooperation of historians and social scientists, which found its expression in the establishment of an interdisciplinary "Center for Studies in Africa, Asia and Latin America" in 1967. This center, working mainly from a comparative perspective on civilizations, developed a truly global perspective once Manfred Kossok, a disciple of Markov and a specialist in modern Latin American history, became the chair. Within a couple of years he transformed the institution into a "Center for the Comparative Study of Revolutions in Modern Times," thus making research on revolutions a central concern of world history in Leipzig during the period from 1974 to 1993.[7]

Both Markov and Kossok revised, rethought, and re-conceptualized world history approaches with new categories inspired by Karl Marx, but this did not lead to a harsh break with traditional narratives. Quite the contrary, seen from today it was part of a constant, eighty-year effort to promote global perspectives on history by stimulating theoretical and methodological considerations of useful research categories and by initiating empirical research from the level of graduate study to broad syntheses. To be sure, the institute never totally replaced other forms of historiography, notably national history, but it always challenged them and created an atmosphere of intellectual competition that led to innovative thinking.

The succeeding directors of the "Institut für Kultur- und Universalgeschichte" published their specific versions of world history, and they did so in different ways: from single-volume monographs to multivolume collections of essays. From an overall perspective, world history turned from a comparative history of civilizations and world regions by Lamprecht to a more culturally based narrative in the case of Walter Goetz; it changed again from a theoretically ambitious history of the decline of Europe by Hans Freyer to the remarkable introduction of non-Western history in Markov's studies on Africa, Asia, and Latin America, only to be once more broadened by Kossok's concept of a world history of revolutions.

When Bruce Mazlish and Ralf Buultjens organized a conference in the late 1980s with the idea of turning traditional concepts of world history into a new practice of global history,[8] Kossok's contributions marked simultaneously the peak of the intellectual developments in Leipzig and the beginning of a new era. After all, this was precisely the time when the "peaceful revolution" of 1989 started in Leipzig, leading to German unification and the implementation of a new political, social and economic order for the former German Democratic Republic. This historical moment could not but challenge world historians in Leipzig to reflect upon and to react on the closely experienced interplay of local events and global developments, which stimulated another round of reconsideration and rethinking of the theory and practice of world history.

The resulting restructuring of the whole university system of Eastern Germany, to conform to the standards and structures of the Federal Republic, brought a serious setback, at least for the efforts of world history. In Western Germany transnational history—not to mention world history—had always stayed at the edges of the academic system, lacking a strong impact on curricula and research structures. This is not to say that national history was not perceived and embedded in transnational narratives ("europäisches Abendland"/ the West, Europe and European integration), but these broader narratives remained implicit, were fragmented, and remained far from being critically reflected.

A first effort in 1992 to return to the institutional heritage of Lamprecht's institute and the interdisciplinary centers—and therefore to the tradition of an independent but integrated structure within the university—was not successful. The president of the "Historikerverband" (Association of German Historians), Wolfgang Mommsen, responded in 1992 to Manfred Kossok that he could only imagine an institute devoted to world history within German academia as part of the Max-Planck-Gesellschaft—a state-founded network of excellent research institutes, independent of the university system. To those familiar with the German academic system, it might be obvious that this would have meant a decisive change, but could also have been a new starting point. But such an endeavor would not come to pass: instead world history in Leipzig was to take a different path.

With the structural renewal of the university, neither was the option of an independent research institute outside of the university discussed nor was an institution within the university seriously considered. World historical perspectives were, however, strengthened through the appointment of several area-studies specialists—in African, Latin American, North American, Near and Middle Eastern, and Comparative Culture history. Their work soon became closely connected with two newly established research institutes: the "Center for the History and Culture of East Central Europe" and the "Simon Dubnow Institute for Jewish History," both associated with the University of Leipzig. These developments steadily increased the potential circle of historians dealing with various aspects of world history. But it was only in 1994, with the founding of the interdisciplinary Center for Advanced Study (CAS), that a stable basis was recreated for intensive collaboration between the individual efforts and the various institutional contexts towards global perspectives.

Graduate Programs and Research: Transnational and Global History

In 2001 the work done at the CAS led to the establishment of an international PhD program in transnational history ("Transnationalization and Regionalization from the Eighteenth Century to the Present"), generously funded by the German Academic Exchange Service (DAAD) with a grant for ten years. The funds were and are still used to develop multidisciplinary curricula and international cooperation, i.e., bringing graduate students from other countries to Leipzig and enriching the teaching program by bringing visiting scholars from abroad. Over the last six years of its existence the program has attracted more than 80 PhD students from over 30 countries, mostly from Eastern Europe, Africa, Asia, and Latin America, although some also arrived from Western Europe and North America.[9] With the CAS as institutional basis, the funding of the DAAD, and the growing number of students, a dynamic of improvement and reworking of the study program evolved, leading to more integrated forms of teaching and to research projects crossing disciplinary boundaries. It soon became visible in research agendas, stimulating new questions and issues.

A first group of such projects was largely devoted to a methodological reflection on theory and practice of world history. These projects examined the basic assumptions, theoretical frameworks, and research categories of world history, and worked on ways of translating them into methods applicable to empirical studies. This interest was accompanied by an intensive and empirically based study of the history of world history writing. With the support of a five-year grant from the European Science Foundation, a collaborative research project took form, relying on a network of European scholars from around 25 countries, and aiming primarily at an examination of the historiographical construction of nations from the nineteenth century onwards. This project deals with regional and transnational alternatives to national history, including traditions of world history writing, and asks in which ways they posed a challenge to the narratives of national history.[10] Other research projects, including several dissertations, are more concerned with the role of area studies within the humanities and social sciences in Europe, particularly from a comparative perspective. Another emphasis in this first group is research on the historiography of empires in various national frameworks and their influence on both national and transnational perspectives. The question that brings all these efforts and projects together is whether or not there are European perspectives on globalization that differ from viewpoints in other regions of the world; and if so, how they historically emerged and what consequences they imply. After all, any kind of international collaboration in the field of world and global history can be successful only in so far as the participants are aware of the differences in intellectual traditions, institutional settings, and also political circumstances.

A second group of research projects historicizes the emergence of different world regions and its current position in processes of globalization. It addresses topics such as "Failing States in Africa," "Transnational Companies in East-Central Europe," and the "Transnational Region of Francophone Countries" with its international organization including areas in Europe, Africa, Asia and the Americas. All studies in this group are characterized by strong collaboration among area-studies specialists at the CAS, to transcend the boundaries of "regions" through a thorough analysis of their construction, looking critically at those colonial and post-colonial perspectives that argue for a fundamental difference between non-Western parts of the world and Western countries. While some early projects started with the problematic assumption that world regions can be taken for granted as a valuable framework of analysis, the debates within the group led to a collective learning process. The result of it was that the curriculum of the PhD program turned increasingly towards constructivist approaches and insights provided by the "spatial turn" in the humanities and social sciences.[11] In practice this means that the analyses do not take spatial categories like nation-states or empires as stable and unchanging entities, but historicize them as products and constructions by concrete historical actors who translate their specific experiences of being in the world into spatial references. These references, or better their claim and contest, are understood as providing for the frameworks for social and symbolical action in both the past and present.[12] Added to that, the basis of the program lies in an understanding of transnational and global history as a field of study that is, on the one hand, interested in flows of people, goods and ideas crossing national borders (interactions as well as entanglements of any kind in human history) but, on the other hand, also tries analytically to understand the emergences of various regimes of territorialization. These regimes are understood as a form of world ordering, which sets the frameworks and determines the condition for any exchange and connectivity. In addition global processes of differentiation and integration, which result from interactions, are understood in these broader terms as representations of territorial orders. In recent years the description and explanation of changes in territorial regimes has become the central focus of the research done in the PhD program: currently, scholars from more than fifteen disciplines work together at the CAS and in the PhD program, trying to expand our knowledge about the spatial construction of empires, nations, or supra-national entities like the EU or Mercosur, thus about the historical emergence of the today's multifold and complex spatial constitution of the world.

In 2006 the PhD program came to be complemented by an interdisciplinary research group and graduate program concentrating on the analysis of "Critical Junctures of Globalization."[13] With funding from the "Deutsche Forschungsgemeinschaft" (German Research Council), twenty PhD students with three-year scholarships work together, aiming firstly at a diachronic comparison of historical and currents conflicts resulting from the changing regimes of territorialization, and secondly at a synchronic comparison of several world regions, among others East Asia, North Africa, and Europe.

In 2006, both the international PhD program in transnational history and the interdisciplinary Research Group on "Critical Junctures of Globalization" became part of a Graduate School, "Understanding Space. Area Studies, Geography, and World History in an age of globalization," within the newly established "Graduate Centre in the Humanities and Social Sciences" of the "Research Academy Leipzig." Two other centers of the Graduate School address the relationship between nomadic and settled (and therefore territorialized) societies and the emergence of new social and transnational spaces within Europe. The "Graduate Center in the Humanities and Social Sciences" at the University of Leipzig seeks decisively to foster its character as a research institution in the field of globalization studies, deriving its particular position from the integration of world and global history, areas studies, and human geography, based on the theoretical assumptions of the "spatial turn." To put the guiding ideas in a nutshell, it can be said that the Graduate Center took as the starting point for its activities the observation that,

> Since 1989, the decline of historical master narratives, the crisis of the nation state and the re-definition of territorial

regimes has troubled history, geography and area studies alike. Because of real-world developments, which have been described by post-modern approaches in terms of an increased 'space-time compression' or as dynamic dialectics between processes of de-territorialization and the search for new forms of re-territorialization, these disciplines are facing major irritations which, in turn, also affect their methodological foundations. The productive nature of these irritations has led to a renewed interest in world history approaches and a re-reading of the relationship between space and territory in different disciplines.[14]

To deal analytically with these developments and irritations, the common notion of spatial entities as containers of individual or collective action was turned into an understanding that conceives them as results of processes of constructing spatial references. With such an actor-centered perspective, social actors again play an active role in the historical creation of spatial orders.

Naturally these assumptions challenge traditional disciplinary perspectives: therefore, responses within the university towards this methodological problematic varied, but in general it encountered interest and a positive reaction. Moreover the support received from a whole range of departments made it possible to implement, at the Graduate Center, a substantially cross-cultural perspective including Western, Central, and Eastern European Studies; South-East and Southern European Studies; as well as Middle East, African, American, and East Asian Studies. It also led to the multi-disciplinary teaching of methods and theories from both the social and cultural sciences. The results will enable the students to bring comparative perspectives together with the study of cultural transfer and interactions.

The Graduate Center also incorporated a M.A. program in "Global Studies." This program was established in 2004 as a European Master's program bringing together the competences of four academic institutions: the London School of Economics and the universities of Wroclaw in Poland, Vienna in Austria, and Leipzig.[15] Students are required to spend their two years of study at two of these institutions, earning a double degree from the chosen partners. Furthermore they can profit from related programs offered at non-European partner universities: the University of California at Santa

Barbara (U.S.), Macquarie University at Sydney (Australia), the University of Dalhousie (Canada) and the University of Stellenbosch (South Africa).

The European Master's program is funded by the European Union Commission with €1.3 million per year, providing grants for students from non-European countries to study in Europe and encouraging European students to study abroad. The number of enrolled students clearly shows that the program is increasingly recognized within and outside of its core countries: while the program started with 36 students, in the second year 54 students were enrolled; now, in the third year the program chairs are confronted with 280 excellent applications from around the world, making entry highly competitive. The fact that more than 60% of the students come from Asia, Africa, the Americas, and Eastern Europe indicates that this particularly European teaching program goes far beyond Europe—in its intellectual perspectives, its student body, and its faculty.

"Global Studies" as concept and teaching program includes world and global history, but history is only one of several disciplinary approaches bound together in the program, integrating research methods from the main areas of the social and cultural sciences and humanities. Although the study programs of the four core institutions differ according to their respective competences, in general the first semester is spent with an introductory unit in global history and a seminar on theories and methods (useful for research on processes of globalization). The next two semesters are devoted to studying in greater detail at least two regions of the world, although the connections among these areas are constantly emphasized in accompanying tutorials and discussion sections. The last semester is filled with the research-oriented master's thesis, but students are also asked to choose between teaching units to gain expertise in economic or cultural aspects of current processes of globalization. The role of world and global history in the program is one of challenging traditional, ahistorical explanations of globalization in teaching the intellectual skills of a radical historicization of the present. How far back in time such an examination goes depends less on general decisions than on the explanatory power of global perspectives for each respective issue and topic. Although the program is still young, it can be said that students have appreciated it, particularly the irritation, the disorder and the intellectual challenge evolving sometimes from conflicting disciplinary perspectives.

These positive experiences and the strong cooperation among all participating institutions suggested seeking contacts with other "Global Studies" programs. During the year 2006 the first exchanges developed, leading in February 2007 to a meeting at the University of California at Santa Barbara which brought the foundation of a Global Consortium in Global Studies.[16] In addition to the already mentioned academic institutions with their respective teaching programs, other institutions from Tokyo, Shanghai and Seoul have now become part of the cooperation. "The purposes of this consortium," as it was agreed upon, "are to promote and facilitate graduate teaching programs in global studies and to foster cooperation among them. The consortium is open to any academic program in the world that offers a graduate M.A., M.Sc., M.Phil., or PhD related to global studies."[17] The first steps of the newly founded Consortium will be to organize the necessary structures for an exchange of curricula and teaching materials, cooperative teaching projects (for example distance learning opportunities), internship opportunities in the countries of the participating universities, student and faculty exchange agreements, and comparative studies on employment areas and career paths of students with this particular education. Ideally these efforts will help to overcome parochialisms inherent in many programs which claim to be global in their outlook, and to create a truly global learning atmosphere for students.

Instruments for Strengthening Teaching and Research

During the last ten years the University of Leipzig has developed into an internationally recognized interdisciplinary center of transnational and global history. Its teaching programs and research groups have stimulated the establishment of two journals and several books series as well as a European-wide organization of scholars interested in this comparatively new field of study.

Among the forums presenting the research done in Leipzig (but also in other places) the academic journal COMPARATIV must be mentioned first. Established in 1991 and published in six thematic issues per year, it has become an important instrument for bringing together perspectives from various disciplines and diverse national contexts. Authors from more than 40 countries have contributed to the ongoing concern of the journal, addressing a range of topics including slave trade, coerced labor, concepts of time and space, gender relations, and environmental policy, to mention only a few.[18] This print journal was supplemented in 2004 by an online forum, "geschichte.transnational" (history.transnational). It is the result of cooperation between the CAS and a research group on "Cultural Transfers" at the Centre National de la Recherche Scientifique, in Paris. Both editors, Michael Espagne and Matthias Middell, together with a German-French editorial group, seek to offer an easily accessible, multi-lingual discussion forum transcending national academic borders and bringing together as many as possible of those working on issues of transnational and global history. Its purposes are to offer rapid publication of new approaches and research results, to create a forum for critical discussions of the increasing number of publications in the field, and to provide an instrument of information about activities. Within the last two years more than 2500 subscribers have expressed their interest in this service, 280 books reviews have been published, and over 300 conferences, workshops and other academic events were brought to wider attention. Moreover, this discussion list conveyed a debate on the potentials, risks and challenges of transnational historical perspectives, in which 22 authors were inspired to comment on a concept of transnational history offered by the two editors of the forum.[19] In 2007 geschichte.transnational and the American-based H-World started to cooperate, providing one step further in turning transnational and global history into an endeavor and practice that reaches beyond established borders and separated academic communities.

In addition to these two journals, since 1994 the CAS has published several books series on various aspects of world history (for example "History of Historiography in the 20th Century" and "Theory and Practice of Studies on Cultural Transfers"), which now total more than 60 collective volumes and monographs. Recently a new series has been launched under the title "Global History and International Studies." Its main aim is to combine the strengths of new scholarship with the needs of an increasing European textbook market. A combination of research and teaching at an advanced level, this series is intended to diminish the prevailing distinction between textbooks and research-based monographs.

In 2002, at a meeting of the summer school of the PhD program in transnational history, the idea of a European organization of scholars dealing with world, global or transnational history arose. It was turned into reality by founding the European Network in Universal and Global History (ENIUGH), which transformed the Karl-Lamprecht-Gesellschaft, an affiliate of the World History Association (WHA), into an international organization based on German legislation for non-profit scientific associations. It was formed as an answer to the rapidly growing interest in world history across Europe and the related demand for efficient structures of cooperation as well as platforms for communication within Europe and with colleagues from other continents. The major aims of the network are: to regularly organize a European congress on themes of world and global history, to publish the periodicals COMPARATIV and "geschichte.transnational" and other research on global linkages from a historical perspective, and to offer administrative help for bi- and multilateral cooperation in the master's and PhD programs.[20]

The First European Congress in World and Global History was held September 22–25, 2005 in Leipzig.[21] The announcement of the conference received much more attention than originally expected: more then 350 participants from all over Europe and overseas met in 47 thematic panels, each with four to six papers. The meetings were accompanied by a book exhibition where more than 50 publishers presented recent publications and thereby made clear that transnational and world history has reached the European book market.[22] The next congress will take place in Dresden in 2008, with "world orders in global history" as its framing theme. The selection of this topic responded to the recent scholarly interest in world orders, i.e. in general patterns and coordinates emerging from the conditions of an entangled and globalized world. The fruitful differences in the ways in which scholars approach and understand world orders are underpinned by the shared observation that the multifold linkages and networks, the connections and mutual influences across the world, both create and are shaped by specific sets of power relations, institutions and ideas. These structures—economic, social, political or cultural—result from conflicts among various claims for and challenges to domination and regulation in contrast to efforts to preserve autonomy and self-control against hegemonic encroachments. Although they are subject to constant change they represent global constellations, which for different periods of time constitute spheres of stability, structures of governance and frameworks of orientation, thus providing order in a complex, incalculable world. So far this research emphasis has been particularly strong in the Anglo-American context, whereas European scholars have rather reluctantly approached this area. Empirical research in many European countries, however, has addressed a whole range of historical situations and developments, which can be bound together to provide insights into world orders. Therefore the second European Congress in World and Global History seeks to bring these potentials together and to discuss their empirical results, focusing on issues of enforcements and contestations of world orders in economic, social, political and cultural spheres. Interpretations of global history are shaped by many disciplines, and so does the understanding of world orders depend on contributions from a wide range of areas in the social sciences and humanities. Therefore the following but not exclusive themes will be under consideration from an interdisciplinary perspective: 1. ideas, conceptualizations and ideologies of world orders, master narratives for its enforcements as well as forms of reaction and resistance against established orders; 2. structures of global governance and in politics and economics (trade, finance, production); 3. labor migration as a challenge to or reinforcement of prevailing international divisions of labor; 4. forms of international cooperation (NGO's, international organizations, transnational networks, multinational corporations); and 5. world orders in areas like literature and art, and in education.[23]

As all these activities show, within the last few years the field of transnational and world history has become a practice that can be found in many places, has led to many forms of transnational collaboration, and has been successful in testing a multi- or even post-disciplinary approach in teaching and research. But as much as these developments simplify, they also complicate the matter. Although it has become comparatively easy today to integrate scholars from different national background into a common endeavor, the translation of the intellectual insights and research results originating in a global scholarly network into local institutional settings has continued to be challenging. During the last ten years, and hopefully also in the future, globally interested historians in Leipzig have been successful in interacting globally while remaining bounded locally. This would have not been possible without the collective effort of many colleagues from various departments; neither could it have been done without the enormous engagement of the graduate students taking the risk of entering a relatively uncertain and unexplored field of education, nor without our partners in Europe and outside. But even as the first milestone is reached, the journey has just begun.

Notes

1. For a comprehensive biography of Lamprecht, see Roger Chickering, *Karl Lamprecht. A German Academic Life 1856–1915* (Atlantic Highlands: Humanities Press, 1993). For a first attempt to compare the German and North American organizational and intellectual environments for the institutionalization of world history, see Matthias Middell and Katja Naumann, "Institutionalisierung der Lehre in Welt- und Globalgeschichte in Deutschland und den USA—ein Vergleich," *Comparativ* 16, 1 (2006): 78–121.
2. On the history of Lamprecht's institute and the context of its foundation, see Matthias Middell, *Weltgeschichtsschreibung im Zeitalter der Verfachlichung und Professionalisierung. Das Leipziger Institut für Kultur- und Universalgeschichte 1890–1990* (Leipzig: Leipziger Universitätsverlag, 2005), vol. 1.
3. A few years later Bernhard Harms in Kiel founded the "Weltwirtschaftsarchiv," while others, including Kurt Breysig in Berlin, were not as successful.
4. On the international influences of Lamprecht's institute see: Luise Schorn-Schütte, "Karl Lamprecht und die internationale Geschichtsschreibung," in *Archiv für Kulturgeschichte* 67 (1985): 417–464; Schorn-Schütte, "Karl Lamprecht weiterdenken," in Gerald Diesener, ed., *Universal- und Kulturgeschichte heute*, (Leipzig: Leipziger Universitätsverlag, 1994).
5. Wolfgang V. Weigand, *Walter Wilhelm Goetz 1867–1958. Eine biographische Studie über den Historiker, Politiker und Publizisten* (Boppard: Boldt Press, 1992). The original *Propyläen* was a periodical published by Johann Wolfgang von Goethe and Heinrich Meyer, 1798–1801.
6. Hans Freyer, *Weltgeschichte Europas*, 2 vols. (Wiesbaden: Dieterichsche Verlagsbuchhandlung, 1948; 2nd edition: Stuttgart: Deutsche Verlagsanstalt, 1954). On Freyer, see Jerry Z. Muller, *The Other God That Failed: Hans Freyer and the Deradicalization of German Conservatism* (Princeton: Princeton University Press, 1987).
7. In addition to a collection of eleven volumes on comparative history of revolutions and a textbook on world history from the fifteenth century to the early twentieth century, see the articles collected in Manfred Kossok, *Ausgewählte Schriften*, vol. 1, *Kolonialgeschichte und Unabhängigkeitsbewegung in Lateinamerika*; vol. 2. *Vergleichende Revolutionsgeschichte der Neuzeit*; vol. 3. *Zwischen Reform und Revolution: Übergänge von der Universal- zur Globalgeschichte* (Leipzig: Leipziger Universitätsverlag, 2000).
8. Manfred Kossok, "From Universal History to Global History," in Bruce Mazlish and Ralph Buultjens, eds. *Conceptualizing Global History*, (Boulder, CO: Westview, 1993), 93-111.
9. For more information on the program see: www.uni-leipzig.de/zhs.
10. www.uni-leipzig.de/zhsesf/; see also Matthias Middell and Lluis Roura y Aulinas, "Challenging the national history paradigm. Remarks on the 'spatial other' in European historiography," *Storia della Storiografia* 50 (2006), 99–116.
11. Constructivist approaches reacted as part of the criticism of linear and large-scale master narratives as framework for historical research and historiography, and argued—whether

consciously or not—for a fragmentation of overall narratives that would open up for a much more differentiated and inclusive perspective of the past. With this they provided the basis for the spatial turn, i.e. the challenge of the historian's former concentration on time and his ignorance of space as a similar complex process. A common ground of its theoretical assumptions is to understand "space" as a process of the "restless formation and reformation of geographical landscapes" and therefore to challenge oversimplified spatial categories and seemingly stable divisions like East/ West, the three worlds, or North/ South. Quote from: David Harvey, "The Geopolitics of Capitalism," in: Derek Gregory and John Urry, eds., *Social Relations and Spatial Structures* (London: Macmillan, 1985), 105. A more elaborate discussion of these issues can be found in Matthias Middell, " Die konstruktivistische Wende, der *spatial turn* und das Interesse für die Globalisierung in der gegenwärtigen Geschichtswissenschaft," in *Geographische Zeitschrift* 93 (2006), 33–44.

12. Very useful contributions for understanding the mechanisms of historically specific results of the construction of space have been formulated by Charles Maier, "Consigning the 20th Century to History. Alternative Narratives for the Modern Era," *American Historical Review* 105 (2000): 807–831; and Jacques Revel, *Jeux d'echelles. La micro-analyse à l'expérience* (Paris: Gallimard-Le Seuil, 1996).

13. The director of this research group is Ulf Engel, professor of contemporary African politics. The teaching staff includes scholars from a range of fields and departments: Japanese Studies, Political Science, Sociology, East-Central European History, African History, Geography, Economic History, and Global History. For further details: www.uni-leipzig.de/zhs/bruchzonen. For an elaborated discussion of the research category, "critical junctures of globalization," see Ulf Engel and Matthias Middell, "Bruchzonen der Globalisierung, globale Krisen und Territorialitätsregimes—Kategorien einer Globalgeschichtsschreibung," *Comparativ* 15, 5–6 (2005): 5–38.

14. Research Plan of the Graduate Centre in the Humanities and Social Sciences at the Research Academy Leipzig (2006), p. 1.

15. For more details on the European Master's program, see its website at www.uni-leipzig.de/zhs.

16. The following institutions participated: the London School of Economics, the universities of Wroclaw in Poland, Vienna in Austria, Stellenbosch in South Africa, and Leipzig in Germany, as well as the University of California, Santa Barbara (USA).

17. Global Consortium in Global Studies, Statement of Purposes, Santa Barbara 2007 (Ms.), p. 1.

18. For an exhaustive bibliography of all the articles and book reviews published since 1991, see the brochure, "10 Jahre Karl-Lamprecht-Gesellschaft" (Leipzig: Leipziger Universitätsverlag, 2002). In the near future all articles from 1991–2005 will be online at www.comparativ.net.

19. www.geschichte-transnational.clio-online.net/forum; the debate took place between January 2005 and March 2007; contributions to this debates came from Volker Berghahn (New York), Andreas Eckert (Berlin/ Cambridge), Ekaterina Emeliantseva (Zurich), Michel Espagne (Paris), Ulrike Freitag (Berlin), Eckhardt Fuchs (Mannheim), Adrian Gerber (Zurich), Christan Gerlach (Pittsburgh), Michael Geyer (Chicago), Peter Haslinger (München/ Regensburg), Ingo Heidbrink (Bremerhaven/Norfolk), Hartmut Kaelble (Berlin), Isabella Löhr (Leipzig), Barbara Lüthi (Basel), Jochen Meissner (Leipzig), Hans-Heinrich Nolte (Hanover), Alexander Nützenadel (Köln), Klaus Kiran Patel (Berlin), Michel Pauly (Luxembourg), Margrit Pernau (Erfurt/ Bielefeld), Dominic Sachsenmaier (Santa Barbara/ Durham), Pierre Yves Saunier (Lyon), Hannes Siegrist (Leipzig), Eva-Maria Stollberg (Bonn), Matthias Middell (Leipzig), Katja Naumann (Leipzig).

20. For further information see: www.eniugh.org
21. The steering committee for the congress comprised: Carol Adamson (Stockholm), Ida Blom (Bergen), Cathérine Coquery-Vidrovitch (Paris), Margarete Grandner (Vienna), Frank Hadler (Leipzig/ Berlin), Miroslav Hroch (Prague), Attila Melegh (Budapest), Matthias Middell (Leipzig), Patrick Karl O'Brien (London), Edoardo Tortarolo (Turin), Peer Vries (Leiden), Susan Zimmermann (Budapest), and for the hosting institution Katja Naumann and Hannes Siegrist (University of Leipzig).
22. For detailed reports on most of the panels and an overall description of the conference see the special thematic issue of *Historical Social Research* (Cologne) 31, 2 (2006).
23. The steering committee consists of scholars from various European countries and includes: Gareth Austin (London School of Economics and Political Sciences), Carol Adamson (Stockholm), Margarete Grandner (University of Vienna), Frank Hadler (Centre for the History and Culture of East Central Europe at the University of Leipzig), Miroslav Hroch (Charles' University, Prague), Marcel van der Linden (International Institute of Social History Amsterdam), Attila Melegh (Central European University Budapest), Matthias Middell (University of Leipzig), Patrick O'Brien (London School of Economics and Political Sciences), Diego Olstein (Hebrew University of Jerusalem), Kapil Raj (EHESS Paris), Shalini Randeria (University of Zurich), Eric Vanhaute (University of Gent), Peer Vries (University of Leiden). For more information visit: www.eniugh.org/congress.

CHAPTER 7

Global History and Economic History: A View of the L.S.E. Experience in Research and Graduate Teaching

Gareth Austin[1]

World history is sometimes said to be the interaction of the global and the local; this chapter presents an academic example. It offers a personal account of the participation of economic historians at the London School of Economics and Political Science in an appropriately inter-continental enterprise, the development of a truly global historiography of material life, and of ways of reflecting and using this in graduate teaching. The project, both at LSE and in general, is still very much in progress. But in its first decade in London it has advanced far enough for one to ask whether there are lessons of more general interest to be extracted from this particular experience, and to consider where we, locally and globally, might go from here. The essay has three main parts. The first, intended for readers wondering what global economic history is about, outlines its provenance and illustrates its major debates. The second briefly narrates the principal institutional initiatives in thinking, teaching, researching, and projecting global history at, or closely involving, the LSE's Economic History Department. These initiatives include the establishment of the first master's degree in global/world history in the United Kingdom, the foundation of the *Journal of Global History*, and the proposal and coordination of a Global Economic History Network. All involve interaction and often partnership with colleagues elsewhere in Britain, other parts of Europe, and across several continents. As the degree and the journal illustrate, this involvement increasingly goes beyond a strictly economic approach to world history. The final section considers the outcomes of these initiatives so far, and the implications for the future.

The New Global Historiography of Material Life

It is fair to say that a new literature has emerged, naturally with precursors and building on assorted older foundations, but mainly within the last twenty years. As usual with historiographical shifts, it can be seen partly as responding to contemporary historical processes, in this case particularly the dramatic spread of Asian industrialization beyond Japan, the growing fears of environmental disaster on a world scale, and the market-integrating dimension of recent "globalization." But the intellectual roots of the new historiography are deeper, for it was made possible by the accumulation of evidence from the preceding several decades of research. Especially important was research on the history of various parts of Asia and Africa before colonization and gunboat diplomacy,[2] which collectively pointed to the conclusion that market behavior (of kinds familiar to economic theorists) and even economic growth were far from being a European innovation. Over the last two decades or so, the logic of research and debate interacted with the growing readiness of many contemporaries to think of themselves in world terms. Such interaction was arguably exemplified in the increased interest in exploring the variations and changes in gender, in slave and free labor, and other aspects of social organization over a long term and global range. This emergent historiography, characterized by the exploration of comparisons and connections on a world scale, already has many strands. For illustration I will highlight four key areas of research and debate.

The first is the contribution of human activities to change in the physical environment. Major syntheses of this history, world-wide, have recently been offered for different periods.[3] This rapidly growing literature offers more than narratives of degradation (though there are, necessarily, plenty of those). There are stimulating syntheses of the interactions between our species and the environment over the extremely long term.[4] There is also vigorous discussion about economic, political, and cultural elements in the causes of man-made environmental change, and the record of constructive responses to this.[5] A controversial theme in some of the writings is the primacy of unequal power, notably organized in states, in bringing about environmental changes and also in promoting forms of conservation, in both cases often with grave costs to less powerful—but resistant—populations.[6]

Second, contemporary "globalization" has prompted inquiry into earlier phases of market integration (and disintegration) on a global scale, whether these phases reflected technological and/or institutional changes. The debate over "when was globalization" obliges historians, economists, and historical sociologists to consider more carefully which kind of international connections they have in mind, and how global they have to be. Such reconsideration has led to new portrayals of the commercial network of the Islamic world of the early modern period; the European establishment of trade links across the oceans, from the fifteenth century; and the partial integration of markets for labor, land, and capital from the late nineteenth century to the outbreak of the First World War.[7] Some writers contend that "world systems" can be traced back to 5,000 years ago.[8] A further dimension of the debate is the role of "world orders," including formal and informal empires and the contemporary international financial institutions, in promoting or restricting international flows of goods and resources.[9]

A third theme is the origins of industrialization. By 1990 a new perspective on the British industrial revolution, and on Western industrialization generally, had begun to emerge from the recognition (derived from the revisionist research on Asian and African history mentioned above) that the world on the eve of the industrial revolution contained a number of centers of market activity, at least some of which had exhibited recurrent (though usually not continuous) real economic growth per head of population.[10] Kenneth Pomeranz and others have revisited the "European miracle," arguing that what he calls *The Great Divergence* in economic fortunes between West and East occurred only after 1750. Moreover, Pomeranz insists, it was based to a large extent on factors that were not part of the internal dynamism of European economies as such: the availability of coal, and—thanks to colonization—of the cultivable resources of the New World, which enabled Britain to escape the resources bottleneck which ultimately stifled the expansion of the Yangzi Valley economy.[11] Alongside Pomeranz's thesis can be set others which, for India, challenge the assumption that Britain in particular and western Europe in general was already economically ahead of Asia by the beginning of the eighteenth century;[12] or which insist upon the decisive importance of the creation of an Atlantic economy, centered on the transportation of African slaves to the New World and their use to produce commodities there, in explaining the precocity of British industrialization.[13] These major works have in turn inspired continuing controversy about the causal relationships and the levels of productivity and real wages in different parts of Eurasia before the industrial revolution began. Most importantly, the debate is fueled by a steady flow of new research, much of it quantitative.[14] Meanwhile Kaoru Sugihara has extended the re-thinking of the traditional Eurocentric account of industrialization. Distinguishing Western "capital-intensive" and Asian "labour-intensive" paths of very long-term economic development, he argues that the diffusion of industrialization to East Asia and other parts of the non-Western world owed much to the adaptation of Western technology to the particular resource endowments of other regions.[15]

A fourth theme is the effects of the various European overseas empires on the economic development of the colonies, before and after their eventual independence. An influential debate, initially among North American economic historians but now spreading more widely, concerns whether the greater economic success of North America over Latin America after their independence from colonial rule should be attributed primarily to differences in resource endowments, or to differences in the respective institutional legacies of British and Iberian rule.[16] On an even wider geographical scale, econometric papers by Daron Acemoglu, Simon Johnson and James Robinson argue that the dramatic divergences in relative prosperity today among Europe's former colonies in the other five continents are largely attributable to whether Europeans settled in large numbers, bringing with them growth-promoting institutions; or whether the Europeans contented themselves with merely extracting revenue while governing at arm's length, in which case the economic results for the territories concerned were relatively adverse.[17] So far their work has been highly influential among economists, but little read by historians. This is unfortunate, because the important debate that is developing from their argument needs to be more fully illuminated by the rich historiography on colonial policies and their economic consequences in different times and places.

We will return to the state of the literature later, having first reviewed the development of the field in London, focusing on forums of various kinds, and on graduate teaching as well as research.

Global History in London

In London, global history began as an experiment and became a mission. The project began with a step which in retrospect seems modest and obvious, but at the time was innovative and even radical: the creation of a regular seminar in such a seemingly amorphous "subject" as "Global History in the Long Run." This was convened (under that title) at the University of London's Institute of Historical Research by the Institute's then director, Patrick O'Brien, and Alan Milward, who at that time held the chair of economic history at LSE. At the inaugural meeting, in February 1996, O'Brien defined the purpose of the seminar in terms which, to academics, almost contradict the notion of a seminar: not as research, but as a conversation among specialists in different fields. As we will see, from this beginning, new research initiatives were to develop later. Throughout the later 1990s, the conversation flowed: in the seminar room, and more widely and perhaps even more fruitfully, over dinner afterwards. The whole exercise in transcending specialisms of period and area was funded by the appropriately-named Renaissance Trust, established by Gerry Martin. After a successful career as an inventor, Martin hoped to learn some clear answers to big questions about the sources of material progress on a meta scale. The first series of meetings considered existing major contributions to the field, starting with a paper by Alan MacFarlane (Cambridge) on Braudel's contribution to global history. Later years focused on "technological progress," "food production systems and their connections to long-term material progress," David Landes's *Wealth and Poverty of Nations* (critiqued by specialists on various regions), the effects of European imperialism on the economic development of early modern Europe, and the significance of markets in long-term economic development and divergence.[18]

In 2000, O'Brien retired as convener of the seminar series. By now a consensus had on some points emerged among the participants, while on others the debate was most likely to be taken further by more detailed consideration and more detailed evidence, much of it new, and involving still wider participation. In organizational terms, the logical next step was to move from seminars to conferences; O'Brien and the Renaissance Trust had already begun to run a series of small residential conferences, featuring papers on a range of individual countries and regions, as well as generalizing essays. These led on to the Global Economic History Network, of which more below.

In London the Institute of Historical Research hosted a second coming of its seminar in global history in 2003–2005, now ranging more widely over political, economic and cultural themes, and led by Felipe Fernandez-Armesto (Queen Mary College, now at Tufts) with funding for visiting speakers provided by Pergammon Press. Meanwhile at LSE a seminar specifically devoted to Global Economic History was founded in 2004 and has run regularly since, in the first term of the academic year.

LSE economic historians had consistently constituted the largest contingent among the participants in the original seminar at the Institute of Historical Research. The thought and discussion it stimulated among us led to three major initiatives at LSE: the introduction of a graduate teaching program in global history, the creation of a new journal, and the establishment of an intercontinental research network. It is most convenient to outline them in reverse chronological order.

The Global Economic History Network (GEHN) could be seen as a globalization of the earlier seminar. Proposed and coordinated by O'Brien from LSE, GEHN was funded by a generous grant from the Leverhulme Trust in Britain, a charitable foundation keen to support major international collaboration in developing fields of intellectual endeavor. Institutionally, it was a partnership between LSE, Osaka University, Leiden University, and University of California, Irvine. There was also a wider network of nearly fifty individual members, from twenty-nine universities in eleven countries, representing five disciplines. The Leverhulme grant provided for a dozen small conferences, which were held in ten countries from September 2003 to December 2006. These gatherings brought together GEHN members and many other scholars. They explored five major themes: the relationships between state formation and markets; imperialism and colonialism; economic cultures; cotton textiles as a global industry; and science, technology, and "useful knowledge." For cotton textiles, the grant also financed new research, through a postdoctoral fellowship and a PhD studentship. The textile research was energetically led by Giorgio Riello, as postdoctoral fellow.[19] At the time of writing a whole set of tightly-edited volumes of revised (and some new) papers is in preparation. The Leverhulme grant permitted a great burst of scholarly production; and also laid the foundation for further collaborative work. The GEHN network is out there, and various research initiatives are being explored. As with the original

London seminar in 2000, when the Leverhulme grant reached its full term at the end of 2006, the time had come for a shift in emphasis: now from conferences towards a greater focus on new research.

The proposal to create a new journal was motivated by a belief that an emerging field needs journals dedicated to it in order to provide a regular forum specifically devoted to encouraging and disseminating work in that area. The admirable *Journal of World History* had already blazed the trail, but there was clearly room for more than one journal. The newcomer would be differentiated from *JWH* partly by a rather greater—but far from exclusive—emphasis on material history. It would combine critical surveys on key issues with the presentation of new research. The proposal was developed by Austin and O'Brien from LSE, and "Tom" (B. R.) Tomlinson from the School of Oriental and African Studies (SOAS), London; always encouraged by the LSE Publications Officer, Beverley Friedgood. Against a background of general decline in subscriptions to academic journals, especially in the vital U.S. market, Ella Colvin of Cambridge University Press believed that there was indeed space for a new journal. The proposal was revised and refined in the light of the feedback from CUP's rigorous review process. Finally, after numerous meetings and memoranda, innumerable emails, and several years, the journal came into existence. It is owned by LSE and published by CUP. The first editors are William Gervase Clarence-Smith (SOAS), Kenneth Pomeranz (University of California, Irvine) and Peer Vries (Leiden). The first volume was published in three issues during 2006.

In 2000 the Economic History Department at LSE admitted the first students to its M.Sc. Global History, the first master's degree program in world history to be offered in the United Kingdom at least. Professor O'Brien, having retired from the Institute of Historical Research, was recruited by the LSE just in time to welcome the first students. The new degree embodied the belief that global history, when focused on a manageably coherent central theme such as material progress, was an approach and a subject that should be shared with students.

The program was designed to offer a closely-knit package of complementary courses, introducing the student to the major debates and issues in the literature, and inviting her to think about the challenges and needs of this exciting field. Each student took two full-year compulsory courses and wrote a 10,000-word dissertation. There was also a compulsory first-term approaches and methods course, followed in the second term by an optional course, chosen from a small selection. The pair of full-year courses addressed—and address—the periods 1000–1800 and 1800 to the present. "Pre-modern paths of growth: East and West compared" enables students to compare the economic trajectories of China and Western Europe up to the era of the industrial revolution. "The development and integration of the world economy" examines modern globalization and the uneven diffusion of industrialization. Meanwhile the approaches course introduced the general field, methods and pitfalls of global history, illustrating them as far as possible with themes (such as environment, empires, and slavery) that are very important in the global historiography but which received less attention in the other courses. At the beginning of the program, intellectual coherence was achieved at the cost of restricted choice. Besides the dissertation topic, the student's only big choice was that of the second-term option, and even then the menu available in any one year was usually short. Still, the topics were diverse, including Nick Crafts' "International economic institutions since World War I,"[20] Janet Hunter's "Gender, work and industrialization," O'Brien's "Scientific, technical and useful knowledge from Song China to the industrial revolution," and Kent Deng's "Shipping and sea power in Asian Waters, c. 1600–1860."

From the first, the M.Sc. Global History was intended to attract, along with economics majors, students who had done little or no economics in their first degree. This was signaled by the department's decision not to insert the word "Economic" in the title of the degree. Correspondingly, the courses that made up the program were meant to be less technical, in terms of quantitative methods and economic theory, than the more arduous (in this respect) of our regular economic history courses. The outcomes, in the first few years anyway, were rather mixed. But there has been important progress in making the program genuinely more friendly for students without much background in economics. When the other history department at LSE, International History, decided to offer a course on "Empire, Colonialism and Globalization" for a new master's degree that it was going to run jointly with International Relations, we took the opportunity to seek their cooperation. The result is that M.Sc. Global History students are allowed to take that course as an alternative to one of the full-year global history courses taught in the Economic History Department. Again, expansion in the Department, which has particularly strengthened its capacity in Asian economic history,[21] among other developments, also allowed the recruitment of a specialist in the history of health. It is intended that Patrick Wallis's course on epidemics in world history will be offered to global historians, as a major step in extending the content of this program in the history of material life beyond the concentration on economic growth. These, and further initiatives, will consolidate the appeal of the degree to students who see economic history as the core, but not the sum, of their graduate training in global history.

Recruitment of students from more diverse disciplinary backgrounds has been assisted recently by the LSE's participation in a consortium of universities, within the European Union's Erasmus Mundus program, to offer a two-year MA degree in Global Studies: A European Perspective. The consortium is coordinated by Matthias Middell and his colleagues at the University of Leipzig and also includes the universities of Wroclaw and Vienna.[22] These students can take the LSE one-year master's program in Global History as either the first or second year of their MA in Global Studies.

In developing the M.Sc Global History, the biggest pedagogic problem concerned the dissertation: what could and should a master's dissertation in global history look like? The outcome was to offer students a choice. They can use primary sources and write about one (or more) specific historical experience(s), providing that they frame the dissertation explicitly as a case-study of a broader theme in the global history literature and discuss their conclusions in relation to that literature. Alternatively, they can write a critical survey of the secondary literature on a particular issue in global history. Some fine dissertations have been produced (among the topics my personal favorite was a comparative study of the political economy of piracy in the seventeenth-century Caribbean and the nineteenth-century South China Sea). Several of the best dissertations were published in the GEHN Working Paper series, and one, suitably revised after the author had moved on to PhD work at SOAS, was developed into a journal article.[23] LSE is dedicated to research-led teaching; as the latter example shows, the global history experience shows mutually beneficial interaction among reflection, synthesis, teaching, and new empirical research.

The Future: The Challenge of Reciprocal Comparison

When the LSE Economic History Department considered the proposal for a master's in Global History, not one member of the department, including myself as proposer, regarded ourselves as global historians. A decade later a large proportion of the department regularly thinks in "global" terms, at least a large part of the time. This is partly because of writing papers for global history seminars and conferences, partly because of devising lectures and courses in the field, and partly because of the mutually-reinforcing effect of discussions with students and colleagues who were also beginning to think in these terms. Again, the department's current PhD students include two representatives of what must be the first generation to approach their specialist research in economic history after master's-level training in global history. This is very different from the trajectory that their elders followed, of learning to think globally only long after the PhD. Meanwhile, the globalizing of economic history has been evident for some years in the subjects of research projects and published articles. It was apparent in the March 2006 editions of the biennial European Social Science History Conference in Amsterdam, and the (then) four-yearly International Economic History Association Congress in Helsinki in September. It was announced that for the IEHA's next congress the title of the meeting is to be changed from "international" to "world." Within the LSE, a proposal was seriously considered to make compulsory, for students taking the M.Sc. Economic History, one of the courses originally created specifically for the M.Sc. Global History. (The course in question was the one on the world economy since 1800.) This was on the grounds that economic history as a subject is now global, and this should be reflected in the compulsory part of master's students' training. Ironically, the "globalization" of the M.Sc. Economic History program has already gone far, in terms of adopting most of the Global History courses as options, and in the revised content of some of the courses specific to the Economic History program.

This trend, local and international, raises questions about the best way to conceive both global economic history and economic history as such. In my view economic history cannot be reduced to the global approach to it. The majority of history articles and books will probably continue to be primarily of interest to students and scholars specifically concerned with the part of the world concerned. Such works will often benefit from being placed in a broad comparative historiography, but the specifically global literature is often only part of that. Conversely, at its most distinctive, and where it adds most to our general understanding of economic history and thereby of economic behavior, global history is defined less by subject matter than by method—the commitment to worldwide comparison and connection of specifically reciprocal kinds. Global history has already brought new ideas and new evidence to the economic historiography; it offers graduate students a revealing perspective on the past and on whichever subjects they did for their first degrees.

But it needs to go further in implementing the ambition of reciprocal comparison. Challenging the one-sidedness of Eurocentric traditions of world history has been much more common with regard to connections (and agency, in the sense of the responsibility for change) than to comparisons. For in the latter context, this one-sidedness is insidiously reinforced by the fact that most of the analytical tools which historians have to think with were derived from, or constructed with reference to, Western historical experience.[24] One of the basic tasks for global history, economic and otherwise, is to make comparisons between Europe (or parts of it) and other regions genuinely "reciprocal," in the sense of "viewing both sides of the comparison as 'deviations' when seen through the expectations of the other, rather than leaving one as always the norm."[25] Besides its analytical merit, this approach can help universities in what many—now more than ever—regard as their wider educational task of helping us all to include a sense of global citizenship among the multiple identities we each embody.

Notes

1. This chapter has benefited from comments on the draft by my departmental colleague Patrick O'Brien, and thoughts on the graduate student experience in global history from Ashley Millar and Albane Forestier. Any mistakes are mine.
2. Starting with Thomas C. Smith on Tokugawa Japan: Smith, *The Agrarian Origins of Modern Japan* (Stanford: Stanford University Press, 1959).
3. John R. McNeill, *Something New Under the Sun: An Environmental History of the Twentieth Century* (London: Allen Lane, 2000); John F. Richards, *The Unending Frontier: An Environmental History of the Early Modern World* (Berkeley: University of California Press, 2003).
4. Jared Diamond, *Guns, Germs and Steel: A Short History of Everybody for the Last 13,000 Years* (London: Chatto & Windus, 1997); David Christian, *Maps of Time: an Introduction to Big History* (Berkeley: University of California Press, 2004).

5. Alfred W. Crosby, *Ecological Imperialism: The Biological Expansion of Europe, 900–1900* (Cambridge: Cambridge University Press, 1986); Robert W. Harms, *Games Against Nature: an Eco-cultural History of the Nunu of Equatorial Africa* (Cambridge: Cambridge University Press, 1987); William Beinart and Peter Coates, *Environment and History: the Taming of Nature in the USA and South Africa* (London: Routledge, 1995); Richard Grove, *Green Imperialism: Colonial Expansion, Tropical Island Edens and the Origin of Environmentalism, 1600–1800* (Cambridge: Cambridge University Press, 1995).
6. Ted Steinberg, "Down to Earth: Nature, Agency, and Power in History," *American Historical Review* 107 (2002): 798–820; Richards, *Unending Frontier*.
7. Kevin H. O'Rourke and Jeffrey G. Williamson, *Globalization and History* (Cambridge, MA: MIT Press, 1999); A. G. Hopkins, ed., *Globalization in World History* (London: Pimlico, 2002); Dennis R. Flynn and Arturo Giráldez, "Path Dependance, Time Lags and the Birth of Globalization," *European Review of Economic History* 8 (2004): 81–108; Jürgen Osterhammel and Niels P. Petersson, *Globalization: A Short History*, trans. Dona Geyer (Princeton: Princeton University Press, 2005; German original 2003).
8. Andre Gunder Frank and Barry K. Gills, eds., *The World System: Five Hundred Years or Five Thousand?* (London: Routledge, 1993); Andre Gunder Frank and Barry K. Gills, "The Five Thousand Year World System in Theory and Praxis," in Robert A. Denemark, Jonathan Friedman, Barry K. Gills and George Modelski, eds., *World System History: The Social Science of Long Term Change* (London: Routledge, 2000), 3–23.
9. Hopkins, *Globalization and History*; Deepak Lal, *In Praise of Empires: Globalization and Order* (London: Palgrave Macmillan, 2004); Jack Goldstone, Review of Deepak Lal, *In Praise of Empires*, EH.Net (2006); Craig Calhoun, Frederick Cooper, and Kevin W. Moore, eds., *Lessons of Empire: Imperial Histories and American Power* (New York: New Press, 2006).
10. E. L. Jones, *Growth Recurring: Economic Change in World History* (Oxford: Oxford University Press, 1988); Patrick Karl O'Brien, "The Reconstruction, Rehabilitation and Reconfiguration of the British Industrial Revolution as a Conjuncture in Global History," *Itinerario* 24 (2000): 117–134.
11. Kenneth Pomeranz, *The Great Divergence: China, Europe, and the Making of the Modern World Economy* (Princeton: Princeton University Press, 2000).
12. Prasannan Parthasarathi, "Rethinking Wages and Competitiveness in the Eighteenth Century: Britain and South India," *Past & Present* (1998): 158, 79–109.
13. Joseph E. Inikori, *Africans and the English Industrial Revolution* (Cambridge: Cambridge University Press, 2002).
14. Notably Robert C. Allen, Jean-Pascal Bassino, Debin Ma, Christine Moll-Murata, and Jan Luiten van Zanden, *Wages, Prices and Living Standards in China, Japan and Europe, 1738–1925* (2005), www.iisg.nl/hpw/factormarkets.php; and Stephen Broadberry and Bishnupriya Gupta, "The Early Modern Great Divergence: Wages, Prices and Economic Development in Europe and Asia, 1500–1800," *Economic History Review* 59 (2006): 2–31.
15. Kaoru Sugihara, "The East Asian Path of Economic Development: A Long-term Perspective," in Giovanni Arrighi, Takeshi Hamashita and Mark Selden (eds), *The Resurgence of East Asia: 500, 150 and 50 Year Perspectives* (London: Routledge, 2003), 78–121.
16. Stanley L. Engerman and Kenneth L. Sokoloff, "Factor Endowments, Institutions, and Differential Patterns of Growth among New World Economies," in S. Haber, ed., *How Latin America Fell Behind* (Stanford: Stanford University Press, 1997), 260–304; John H. Coatsworth, "Economic and Institutional Trajectories in Latin America," in John H.

Coatsworth and Alan M. Taylor, eds., *Latin America and the World Economy since 1800* (Cambridge MA: Harvard University Press, 1998), 23–54; Douglass C. North, Barry R. Weingast, and W. Summerhill, "Order, Disorder and Economic Change: Latin America versus North America," in B. Bueno de Mesquita and Hilton Root, eds., *Governing for Prosperity* (New Haven: Yale University Press, 2000), 17–58; Regina Grafe and Maria Alejandra Irigoin, "The Spanish Empire and its Legacy: Fiscal Redistribution and Political Conflict in Colonial and Post-colonial Spanish America," *Journal of Global History* 1 (2006): 241–267.

17. For a summary of their thesis in largely non-technical language, see Daron Acemoglu, Simon Johnson, and James A. Robinson, "Institutions as the Fundamental Cause of Long-run Growth," in P. Aghion and S. Dulauf, eds., *Handbook of Economic Growth*, vol. Ia (Amsterdam: Elsevier, 2005), section on "The Reversal of Fortune," pp. 407–21. See also Acemoglu, Johnson, and Robinson, "The Colonial Origins of Comparative Development: An Empirical Investigation," *American Economic Review* 91 (2001): 1369–1401; and Acemoglu, Johnson, and Robinson, "Reversal of Fortune: Geography and Institutions in the Making of the Modern World Income Distribution," *Quarterly Journal of Economics* 118 (2002): 1231–1279. For a short introduction to relevant historiography, see Gareth Austin, "Economic Imperialism," in Joel Mokyr, ed., *Oxford Encyclopedia of Economic History*, Vol. 2 (New York: Oxford University Press, 2003), 145–55.

18. David S. Landes, *The Wealth and Poverty of Nations: Why Some are so Rich and Some so Poor* (New York: Norton, 1998).

19. Who has now been appointed to the University of Warwick's new Global History and Culture Centre, directed by GEHN member Maxine Berg.

20. Which at the time of writing he continues to teach, despite having otherwise moved to the University of Warwick.

21. With the appointment of Tirthankar Roy (India) and Debin Ma (East Asia).

22. For further discussion of this degree program, see Chapter 6 of this volume.

23. Sebastian R. Prange, "'Trust in God, but tie your camel first.' The Economic Organization of the Trans-Saharan Slave Trade between the Fourteenth and Nineteenth Centuries," *Journal of Global History* 1 (2006): 2.

24. Florence Bernault, "L'Afrique et la modernité des sciences sociales." *Vingtième siècle: Revue d'histoire* 70 (2001): 127–38; Dipesh Chakrabarty, *Provincializing Europe: Postcolonial Thought and Historical Difference* (Princeton: Princeton University Press, 2000).

25. Pomeranz, *Great Divergence*, 8; cf. R. Bin Wong, *China Transformed: Historical Change and the Limits of European Experience* (Ithaca: Cornell University Press, 1997).

CHAPTER 8

World History at Washington State University

Healther Streets

When I was first hired at Washington State University in 1998, I did not imagine I would become involved in the field of world history. I was trained as an historian of Britain and the British Empire, and my job description clearly located me as a Europeanist. Yet I found myself in an institutional environment that values and rewards global perspectives in teaching undergraduates (Washington State requires all undergraduates to take two semesters of World Civilizations), and I gradually began to infuse a global dimension into most of my courses. Instead of a course on the British Empire, then, I offered a course on Global Imperialism. Instead of teaching about Britain as an isolated nation, I taught British history in the context of imperial expansion and international rivalries. I also taught World Civilizations each year, and found that I was becoming increasingly aware of—as well as interested in—the literature on world history. As a result, when my department chair asked me to redesign and direct our existing (but nearly defunct) graduate program in world history in 2002, I was willing to take on the challenge even though I knew I still had much to learn about the field.

I must say at the outset that, when I speak to fellow historians about the process of setting up a graduate program in world history, most automatically assume that I must have had to overcome tremendous resistance in my department. This assumption is often accurate, because one of the greatest obstacles to creating such programs certainly lies in resistance at the departmental or college level, and many historians friendly to the idea of world history hope to discover how to surmount such opposition. In my case, however, any resistance to the idea of world history had already been defeated by the time I arrived on the scene, which meant that I was free to construct a program without also negotiating a political and professional minefield. Thus, while my tale here cannot provide a roadmap for how to convince colleagues, chairs, and deans to support world history as a graduate field, I hope instead that it will provide some insight into why world history PhD programs are necessary, how such programs can be structured, the kinds of research they can produce, and their possibilities for future success.

The World History PhD? To Offer or Not to Offer

Although Washington State did have a graduate program in world history on the books prior to 2002, it had only ever had one student and lacked a coherent curriculum. My task, therefore, was not to revive the old program but to reconceptualize it from its very core. Key to this reconceptualization was whether or not we wanted to launch a full-fledged PhD program in world history, or if we wanted to offer world history only as a minor, secondary field. This decision, of course, was fundamental, for it would determine both the scope and size of the program. There were models to follow for both kinds of programs, and I wanted to be sure I knew enough about each before I decided what would be right for Washington State.

As it turned out, all but one of the dozen or so institutions that provided graduate training in world history offered world history only as a minor or supporting field rather than as a PhD. Indeed, Northeastern University in Boston was the only place where graduate students could actually earn a PhD in world history. I hoped that learning the reasons for this would help me design a solid and effective program that would serve both students and faculty members well.

My research into existing programs led me to conclude that faculty members who participated in programs offering World as a supporting field had three primary rationales for such an approach. First, some said it was simply impossible to convince their colleagues, department chairs, or deans that a PhD program in world history was either desirable or viable. Hence, offering World as a supporting field was the only way to provide specialized training within the confines of otherwise traditional or hostile graduate departmental offerings. Second, some firmly believed that today's academic job market was simply not ready for world history PhDs, and that students finishing with such degrees would not be able to be placed. Finally, some felt that world history is a methodological approach rather than a research field, or that it should be offered simply as a teaching field to help graduate students prepare for college survey courses in world history. As such, they argued that World was not truly a viable PhD field.

On the other side, those who advocated World as a major field argued that such an approach was the most effective way to train graduate students to think about historical events using a global perspective from the outset of their graduate careers. Moreover, a major field in World would allow graduate students to carry out globally-oriented research projects that would normally receive little support in history departments divided by national or area specialties. Perhaps most importantly, advocates of this approach argued that PhD programs in world history would emphasize the vitality of the field as a research specialty rather than as a teaching field.

After much deliberation and discussion with my department chair, I decided that Washington State would offer a full-fledged PhD program in world history. While I understood the reservations many historians had about such an approach, my decision was prompted primarily by institutional placement. I had learned, through studying Pat Manning's yearly reports on the World History Center at Northeastern, that institutional support—both intellectual and financial—was vital to a successful program.[1] In my view, and unlike many other departments in the country, I believed we had the right kind of support at Washington State. First, our history department was friendly to the idea of such a program, which alone represented a major advantage in an academic field so often hostile to world history. Second, by creating such a program we could complement Northeastern University's program in the eastern United States with another, similar program on the other side of the country.[2] My hope was that our program—if successful—could recruit from those students who are inclined to live in the western states. Third, when I surveyed our faculty I found that six of my colleagues were willing to teach courses and supervise students within the program. Although my department was supportive of world history, I reasoned that in order to be successful we needed active participation by faculty members with a variety of specializations. With the commitment of six colleagues, I felt we had enough diversity to offer a strong set of courses to potential students. Finally, the dean of the College of Liberal Arts was encouraging, and was open to the idea of new faculty lines in world history.

All the institutional support in the world would mean nothing if I did not also believe in the future of world history as a research field. I have been deeply impressed by the innovative and original contributions self-identified world historians have made to the discipline of history, and I am convinced by the work of new and emerging scholars of the future potential of the field. I also believe—along with Pat Manning—that if we do not provide institutionalized graduate training in world history, the field will eventually fail to thrive. Instead, scholars will continue to come to world history late in their careers, without having had the benefit of formal guidance in the field. Moreover, although only time will tell if this is correct, I believe that the concerns of our own global age are encouraging historians from a wide variety of fields to explore the problems of the past from an increasingly global perspective. As a result, it seems likely that the current trend toward job advertisements that request some kind of global or world expertise—even in clearly-defined national fields—will continue. If the excellent placement rate of Northeastern's world history graduates is anything to go by, the academic job market may well continue to be able to accommodate PhDs with just such global perspectives.

The Program: Structure, Evolution, Cohesion

Once the decision was made to create the PhD program, constructing it was fairly simple. I did not try to reinvent the wheel, but rather borrowed as many good ideas from existing programs as possible. And, since Northeastern was the only full-fledged PhD program and was very successful besides, much of the initial structure of Washington State's program was based on that model. Our program has evolved over time, of course, but I have come to believe that the two most important ingredients to a good program are a strong, well-conceived curriculum and cohesion among the faculty, among the students, and between faculty members and students. Washington State's program is far from perfect, but we have worked hard to improve both our curriculum as well as our sense of group identity over time.

For the first four years our program was in existence, the curriculum for the graduate program was as follows: students prepared a primary field in world history, and then prepared both a secondary regional field and a secondary thematic field (see attached Appendix #1). For the primary field, students were required to take two courses—one on methodology and historiography and one research seminar—in addition to mastering an extensive reading list for the preliminary examination. The regional and thematic secondary fields included both coursework and individualized reading lists, and were meant to support student research into specific geographies, temporalities, and methodological foci.

In 2006, the collective faculty involved in the program realized that the above curriculum was not accurately reflecting our goals for training world historians. Although not all world historians agree on this matter, at Washington State the faculty members involved in the world history program are unanimous in the belief that practicing world history does not obviate the need for regional expertise. This regional expertise does not have to be defined by a national specialization—in fact, we encourage students to conceptualize and to study multi-national regions. Yet we are firm in believing that it is difficult, if not impossible, to ask new or innovative questions about places, times, connections, or change over time without a deep understanding of at least one region. And while we had designed the original program curriculum with such a premise in mind, it became clear to us that the regional aspect of our graduate training was playing second fiddle to the primary field in world history.

In response, we altered the curriculum to emphasize the equality we envision between the field of world history and regional training. Now, students prepare two co-equal fields—one in world history and one in a regional area—and one secondary thematic field. Our goal here is to underline our students' expertise in both fields. Thus, when they complete the program, we intend for them to be fully prepared for positions in either world history or in their regional specializations. This has the obvious benefit of expanding job opportunities for our students, but its main purpose is to demonstrate that world historians need not be generalists: rather, they can think in global terms and yet still possess depth of knowledge.

In addition to the two coequal and one secondary field, in the interests of ensuring increased breadth our students now prepare a non-examination minor in another region, theme, or discipline. Finally, while our students have always been required to have research skills in one language besides English, we now strongly encourage them to have research skills in two other languages. This modified curriculum, we believe, more accurately reflects the emphasis we wish to place on world history as a viable research field. It is emphatically not, as so many unfamiliar with the field have assumed, "history light."

Outside the specific curriculum requirements of the program, world history at Washington State is somewhat uniquely constructed since its faculty and its students are split between two campuses—one in Pullman, the other in Vancouver—on opposite sides of the state. Although there are some clear potential disadvantages to this situation, computer technology has in fact allowed our split campuses to become an asset to the program. For one thing, it allows us to recruit graduate students at both locations. This is advantageous because while Pullman is WSU's main campus, it is nevertheless located in an isolated area of eastern Washington. Vancouver, in contrast, is in an urban location very close to Portland, Oregon. By having the two campuses, then, we can appeal to a wide variety of potential students. We can also offer our students the opportunity to experience both kinds of campus life by moving between the campuses at different times in their graduate career.

Our split campuses also model the very global, technology-based world which has helped give rise to the burgeoning interest in world history in the first place. Washington State is fortunate to be one of the "most wired" universities in the United States, and its campuses are connected through a system of live-action video classrooms. What this means is that the barriers of geographical space are no longer as cumbersome as they once were: thus, when a faculty member on either campus offers a course in world history, students at the other campus can take the class through the live-action video connections. In the same way, graduate students at either location can come together with faculty members on the other campus through such connections. We now have had extensive experience with multi-campus meetings between graduate students and faculty members for oral examinations and MA as well as PhD defenses, with very positive results. Currently, two of our PhD candidates and one MA student are located in Vancouver, while seven PhD candidates and one MA candidate are located in Pullman. Out of the six faculty members actively involved in the program, two are in Vancouver and four are in Pullman.[3] In 2006-2007, one of our graduate students finished his course work in Pullman and shifted to Vancouver for the research and writing phase of his dissertation. In the future, we hope to see more of this kind of movement among both the students and even among the faculty.

From the very beginning, part of the structure of the world history program has been tied to creating a strong sense of cohesiveness among the students and faculty members involved. This, I believe, is nearly as critical as the curriculum itself, because it helps maintain morale and enthusiasm while also creating networks with students and faculty members outside the program. Each month, then, students and faculty members attend a meeting to discuss issues relating to the program, upcoming conferences, and other issues. In addition, the Pullman group hosts monthly social events designed to allow both new and seasoned students and faculty members the chance to interact informally (we haven't yet discovered how to have parties that connect our two campuses). Moreover, each year since 2004, WSU students and faculty members from both campuses have actively participated in the Northwest World History Association conference, which was founded by Candice Goucher, Sue Peabody (both at the Vancouver campus), and myself specifically for this purpose. Indeed, the conference has allowed our students the chance both to present their own work and to meet and talk with well-known world historians (including Pat Manning, David Christian, Judith Zinsser, Peer Vries, and Adam McKeown). Individual graduate students have also taken it upon themselves to foster this sense of cohesiveness on their own time: Maryanne Rhett, a PhD candidate who has just reached the research stage for her dissertation, has recently designed and constructed a dedicated web page (www.wsuworldhistory.com) for the WSU world-history students on both campuses. The net result of all these efforts has produced a real sense of group identity among those involved in the program: not necessarily an easy task in any program, much less one that is split between two campuses.

The Students

One of the reasons for the enthusiasm among the world-history cohort at WSU is the quality of the students. Almost without exception, every student who has been accepted into the program since 2002 has come well prepared and with a clear commitment to world history. Their research projects and activities reflect, I hope, the breadth of training they have received at

WSU, but even more importantly they reflect the vitality, enthusiasm, and ingenuity of the field and of the students themselves.

Among our advanced graduate students, including the two who have completed the program with their PhDs, research projects vary temporally from the medieval period to the twentieth century, and geographically from India to Cuba, Mexico, the British Empire, and the Atlantic and Pacific Worlds. Their subjects are equally diverse: Mary Jane Maxwell, a graduate of the program and current instructor at Penn State University, focused on Christian travelers to the Dar al-Islam in the fifteenth and sixteenth centuries, and was particularly concerned with conversion experiences—real or feigned—to Islam. Some of her findings are already published.[4] Armand Garcia, our most recent graduate from the program, used his interest in Latin American history to explore the transnational dimensions of the nation building efforts of the late nineteenth-century Cuban independence leader José Martí (1853-1895). Although many scholars have explored various aspects of Martí's life and work, none have charted the global origins of his ideas on revolution, religion, violence, and education—a heritage which includes not only Latin America but Europe, the United States, and India. Some of Armand's conclusions were published in the *Latin American Literary Review*, and he has begun a tenure-track appointment at Eastern Washington University.[5]

Among our advanced graduate students currently researching and writing their dissertations, all four are working on aspects of empire and imperialism but in vastly different ways. Amitava Chowdhury investigates the political, cultural and social processes that contributed to the formation of identity among the African and Indian forced-labor diaspora in colonial plantations. He uses a variety of methodological and disciplinary tools to argue that identity is best understood as a result of cultural memory, and cannot be understood simply as a result of individual or social choice or as a result of ethnic and religious processes. Through this project, he links two distinct diasporic groups in both the Atlantic and Pacific worlds in new and intriguing ways. While also working on questions of empire, Maryanne Rhett focuses her research on the creation and legacy of the 1917 Balfour Declaration as a document influenced not only by events in the Middle East, but also by events in other parts of the British Empire as well as in the world more generally. Her goal is to place the document into a global context in order to better understand its significance and to create a clearer picture of the global community as a composite of individual actors, regional pressures, and transregional realities. Aaron Whelchel also focuses on the British Empire, but his concern is with the ideological interactions between the periphery and the core through the lens of imperial education. He is most interested in the ways in which educational ideology was applied to different regions of the Empire, such as Ireland and India, and the impact of the imperial experience on educational practices back in the metropole. His goal is to understand better how educational practices and views on childhood are impacted by imperialism in general. Finally, Mark Moreno looks not at the British but the French Empire, and the ways in which the French intervention in Mexico (1862–1867) impacted the development of Mexican nationalism. More specifically, his research focuses on intersections of international commerce, or the "world system," French ideologies of foreign expansion, and liberal and indigenous ideologies of nationalism and their influence on small communities and renegade groups.

Just as much diversity and enthusiasm exists in the research interests of the PhD candidates who have not yet completed preliminary exams. Cynthia Ross, who completed an MA in 2006 and has now moved on to the PhD program, focuses on World War II and resistance in British Southeast Asia. Paul Fisher's interests are, like many of his world history cohort, with empire, but in this case with the far earlier Roman Empire. Specifically, he hopes to compare Roman imperialism with other contemporary or near-contemporary empires, but he also hopes to draw conclusions about imperial administration that may be relevant for historians of modern imperialism. Barbara Traver and Tess Rond both explore the early modern Caribbean, but in different ways. Barbara hopes to engage the question of the international dimensions of the creation of the racial caste system in Saint-Domingue, while Tess Rond's interests are with gender, slavery, and the law, and especially with connecting experiences globally as well as locally.

These research projects—even those that are in their earliest stages—demonstrate, I believe, how rich and promising world history can be as a graduate research field. The collective work of Washington State's world history graduate students, indeed, is a far cry from what those outside the field have often labeled as generalist. Rather, their research is based on deep regional and thematic expertise, but is unique because of the world-historical questions they bring to their areas of specialization.

Further Development and Future Prospects

Thus far, the program at Washington State has been fortunate to attract such excellent students and to receive so much support from the History Department as well as the College of Liberal Arts. The program has energy, enthusiasm, and enjoys the fruitful collaboration of two distant campuses. The faculty members and students involved in the program feel poised for future growth and developments, and we are actively working toward several specific goals. Primary among those goals is the need for additional faculty hires—particularly in under-represented areas such as African history—to work with what we hope will be increasing numbers of graduate students in the program. While we have six dedicated and involved faculty members, ideally we will have three new faculty lines within the next five years. We have been promised a line in African and world history for the 2007–2008 academic year, which we believe is an encouraging sign. In addition to new faculty members, we are determined to push the boundaries of our multi-campus structure ever further by creating more opportunities for both students and faculty members on both campuses to physically move between the campuses. So far, we are off to a good start: in fall 2006, one of our graduate students was the first to complete coursework on the Pullman campus and then move to the Vancouver campus for the remainder of his graduate career. In fall 2007, the Vancouver campus is offering a teaching-assistant position for a Pullman world history graduate student. Finally, we are actively in search of increased financial support for the program, both internally at Washington State as well as externally, in order to fund graduate research, the creation of a resource center, and the creation of a master's program designed specifically for secondary teachers.

Ultimately, the success of the program will come down to developments in the historical discipline, hard work, and money. It is still too early to tell whether academic job offerings in the near future will call for world historians in the numbers we imagine. Hostility toward world history is still palpable in many quarters, and if the job prospects for world historians are to change that attitude will need to change with it. Part of the answer, of course, is for graduate programs in world history to produce truly excellent PhDs whose research captures the attention of other historical fields. At Washington State, our hope is to do just that in both the near- and long-term. Then there is the question of money. As Pat Manning has argued many times, without institutional investment in the form of new faculty lines and student recruitment, no world history program can survive for long. The signs for such support at Washington State have been promising so far, but it is clear that further and more extensive financial support will be necessary if the program is to continue beyond the tenure of those who founded it. It seems clear that financial support must come from other quarters as well: not just to Washington State but to other universities around the country and around the world. As long as there are only a handful of programs offering PhDs in world history, change will be slow. It is my hope that more historians at a variety of institutions will recognize the potential and the possibilities of world history as a research field to build new, and even better, programs of their own.

APPENDIX

The two documents reproduced below are the Washington State University graduate program regulations for world history as initially adopted in 2002 and as revised in 2007.

1. WORLD HISTORY TRACK, 2002

This supplement is designed for students selecting world history as their Primary Field. It is to be used in conjunction with the History Department's *Graduate Guidelines* and the *Graduate School Policies and Procedures*. Only additions to and exceptions from the traditional graduate program in history are included below.

World History is a methodological and research field based around the study of global problems, events, patterns or issues. Students of World History will master both a primary area of research and a thematic issue that locates the area in its larger global context. The World History program also provides specific training and mentoring in the teaching of world history at the college level.

Master of Arts Program

Program requirements: The M.A. track generally consists of 30 credit-hours beyond the bachelor's degree. Students must fulfill the requirements in the regular M.A. track but must also take History 571, which serves as the field course requirement. The student must secure approval for the thesis topic by the major professor and the Coordinator of World History.

PhD Program

Program requirements: The PhD track consists of 72 credit hours beyond the bachelor's degree. These hours must include History 570 (Topics in World History) and History 571 (World History Theory and Methods) for preparation of a primary field in World History. Students will also prepare two secondary fields; one in a regional area of concentration and the other in thematic global issues.

Primary field: The preliminary exam in the primary field will be prepared by the Coordinator of World History and the major professor. Students are expected to demonstrate mastery of the methodologies, historiographical issues, problems, and approaches that characterize the discipline of world history.

Regional Secondary Field: For one of the two secondary fields, students are expected to master a regional area of concentration, chosen from among the following: [preliminary exams in the secondary field will be prepared and evaluated by at least one professor in each chosen secondary field]

- United States
- Early Europe
- Modern Europe
- Latin America
- Middle East
- Modern East Asia

Thematic Secondary Field: The other secondary field will focus on an inter-regional thematic issue, chosen from among the following:

- Gender
- Environment
- Imperialism
- Warfare/Military
- Atlantic World
- Pacific Rim
- Ancient World
- Race
- Migration/Immigration

The student's committee will consist of the Coordinator, the major professor, and at least one additional professor from each secondary field.

Research: Dissertations for the primary field in World History must explore a thematic global pattern or issue, and must be approved by both the major professor and the Coordinator. The Coordinator must be a member of the Doctoral committee.

Training for Teaching World History at the College Level: Students in World History should TA both sections of World Civilizations at WSU. In conjuction with History 595, World

History students will complete additional pedagogical training—such as lecturing and designing syllabi—specific to the teaching of world history.

2. REVISED WORLD HISTORY TRACK, 2007

PhD Program requirements: The PhD track consists of 72 credit hours beyond the bachelor's degree. These hours must include the following for preparation of the examination field in World History historiography and methodology, which is to be coequal with the regional field.

History 570 (World History Theory and Methods)
History 571 (Topics in World History)

In addition to the coequal examination fields in World History historiography and methodology and the regional field, students will prepare a secondary thematic examination field and a minor non-preliminary exam field of at least 6 credit hours in an additional regional area or theme.

Coequal Historiographical and Methodological field: The preliminary exam in this field will be prepared by the Coordinator of World History and the major professor. Students are expected to demonstrate mastery of the methodologies, historiographical issues, problems, and approaches that characterize the discipline of world history.

Coequal Regional Field: Students are expected to master a regional area of cncentration, chosen from among the following:

- United States
- Early Europe
- Early Modern Europe
- Modern Europe
- Latin America
- Middle East
- Modern East Asia
- South Asia
- Africa
- Atlantic World
- Pacific Rim
- Ancient World

Secondary Thematic Field: Students are expected to master an inter-regional thematic issue, approved by the Coordinator of World History and chosen from among the following topical areas:

- Gender
- Environment
- Imperialism
- Warfare/Military
- Race

- Migration/Immigration
- Class

- Religion
- Cultural Memory Systems

Additional thematic issues can be approved by the Coordinator of World History when appropriate.

The student's committee will consist of the Coordinator, the major professor, and at least one additional professor from each secondary field.

Minor Regional or Thematic Field: Students will prepare a minor, non-prelim field consisting of at least 6 credit hours in any of the above regional or thematic focuses, or in a discipline outside of History.

Research: Dissertations for the primary field in World History must explore a thematic global pattern or issue, and must be approved by the major professor and the Coordinator. The Coordinator must be a member of the Doctoral committee.

Language: Doctoral students earning the PhD in World History must have reading competency in at least one language besides English, although they are strongly encouraged to gain reading competency in two languages.

Training for Teaching World History at the College Level: Students in World History should TA both sections of World Civilizations at WSU. In conjunction with History 595, World History students will complete pedagogical training, such as lecturing and designing syllabi, determined by the Coordinator of World History.

World History as a Secondary Field: Students who wish to pursue World History as a secondary field must take History 570 (World History Theory and Methods) and History 571 (Topics in World History).

A final reading list will be determined by the Coordinator of World History, the professor taken for History 570, and the student. Preliminary Examinations will be written by the Coordinator of World History and the professor taken for History 570. Students will also receive pedagogical training in the teaching of world history in conjunction with History 595.

MA Program requirements: The M.A. track generally consists of 32 credit-hours beyond the bachelor's degree. Students must fulfill the requirements in the regular M.A. track but must also take the following courses

History 570 (World History Theory and Methods)
History 571 (Topics in World History)

History 570 and History 571 will serve as the field course requirements. The student must secure approval for the thesis topic from the major professor and the Coordinator of World History.

Notes

1. For the World History Center annual reports (1995-2004), see www.worldhistorycenter.org, "About Us."
2. As it worked out, however, Manning closed the World History Center at Northeastern in 2004, citing lack of institutional support. Patrick Manning, "Concepts and Institutions for World History: The Next Ten Years," in Manning, ed., *World History: Global and Local Interactions* (Princeton: Markus Wiener, 2005), 232.
3. The Vancouver faculty members include Candice Goucher and Sue Peabody, and the Pullman faculty members include myself, Raymond Sun, Ian Wendt, and Robert Staab.
4. Mary Jane Maxwell, "Afanasii Nikitin: An Orthodox Russian's Spiritual Voyage in the Dar al-Islam, 1468–1475," *Journal of World History* 17 (2006): 243–266.
5. Armand Garcia, "Situating Martí in a Global Context: the *Bhagavad-Gita*'s Wisdom in the Works of Cuba's Preeminent Patriot and Poet" *Latin American Literary Review*, 34, no. 67 (2006): 5–33.

CHAPTER 9

The *Journal of World History*

Jerry H. Bentley

It is a commonplace observation that curricular demands and the needs of classroom teachers have deeply influenced the development of world history. Some even consider world history to be primarily a pedagogical venture rather than a field of basic research and historical analysis.[1] Yet the principal professional organization serving the field, the World History Association (WHA), has proudly and prominently promoted both teaching and research in world history from its earliest days. The WHA constitution specifies that the organization's purpose is "the promotion of studies of world history through the encouragement of research, teaching, and publication" (Article II).[2] The decision to emphasize research alongside teaching was quite deliberate. After the foundation of the WHA in December 1982, a steering committee met at the Wingspread Conference Center in Racine, Wisconsin (18–19 May 1983) to develop a constitution and an institutional structure for the new organization. According to the report of Craig A. Lockard, then serving as WHA secretary pro tem, the constitution proposed by the steering committee "reflects the dual nature of the association, stressing the promotion and facilitation of both scholarship and teaching." During the course of the Wingspread meeting, Lockard and Tien-wei Wu outlined steps that the WHA might take to advance graduate education and scholarly research in world history.[3] Lockard later offered an impassioned plea for the development of graduate programs and research opportunities in world history, and programs for advanced education in world history soon began to emerge.[4]

But what does research mean in the case of world history? For most fields of historical inquiry, the meaning of research has been clear since the emergence of professional historical scholarship in the mid-nineteenth century: basic research has involved the close and critical examination of archival documents and other primary sources that presumably offer the most direct and reliable surviving testimony to the past. Practicing historians know well that this kind of basic research requires mastery of relevant languages and facility with advanced research techniques as well as control over large bodies of scholarly literature. To what extent might the nineteenth-century model of professional historical scholarship transfer to the field of world history?

Founding the *Journal of World History*

If the term *world history* implied that individual historians must deal with the whole history of the whole world, professional historical scholarship as it has developed since the mid-nineteenth century would be impossible for world history—an absolute non-starter. Yet the term *world history* raises expectations that it will deal with something more than just any odd event that happened to have taken place during some past time in some part of the world. How might it be possible to frame an understanding of world history that enables scholars to undertake rigorous basic research while also delivering substance that merits recognition as world history?

This is one of the questions that two groups of historians faced during the years 1987 and 1988 as they planned the foundation of a new scholarly publication, the *Journal of World History* (hereinafter referred to as *JWH*). The first group consisted of scholars at the University of Hawai`i, where in 1985 history faculty had designed and instituted a PhD field in world history. Most active in this group were Professor Daniel W. Y. Kwok, department chair at the time, and myself, with welcome support from others both within and beyond the Department of History. In light of the immediate popularity of the department's new PhD field in world history and the attention that it attracted nationwide, we began in the spring of 1987 to discuss the possibility that the time might be ripe for the establishment of a new scholarly journal to serve as a forum for basic research, analysis, and scholarly reflection on issues of world history. By sheer coincidence, at that same moment the higher administration of the university decided to provide funds to launch several new journals to be published by the University of Hawai'i Press. Following a university-wide competitive review of proposals, the *JWH* became one of four new journals on the Press's list.

The second group of historians who collaborated on the establishment of the *JWH* consisted of members and leaders of the World History Association. Most active in the effort from the WHA side were past president Kevin Reilly, president Arnold Schreier, vice president and president-elect Marilynn Jo Hitchens, and members of the WHA executive council, including most prominently Sarah Shaver Hughes, Ray Lorantas, Lynda Shaffer, and Judith P. Zinsser. As historians in Hawai'i worked with university resources to found a new journal, they consulted with the WHA leadership about the possibility that a new *JWH* might become an official publication of the WHA. Both the Hawai'i group and representatives of the WHA were quite enthusiastic about this prospect. After considering several different models for a relationship, the two groups agreed to a formal affiliation by terms of which the *JWH* became the official journal of the WHA.

The nature of the relationship between the *JWH* and the WHA was not the only issue the two groups of historians faced in 1987 and 1988. More substantively, there was the question: what would the term *world history* mean for purposes of a professional historical journal? Fortunately, the historians who contemplated a new *JWH* were able to draw inspiration from a body of scholarship that had been emerging already for some time, so it was not necessary to invent a brand new understanding of world history. The works of William H. McNeill, L. S. Stavrianos, Marshall G. S. Hodgson, Philip D. Curtin, Andre Gunder Frank, Immanuel Wallerstein, and others offered several different and distinctive but also complementary and sometimes overlapping approaches that served as examples of ways historians might address significant large-scale issues of world history through rigorous scholarly analysis.[5]

On the basis of this scholarship, the founders of the *JWH* decided that for purposes of the new journal, world history would mean studies that explicitly compare historical experiences across the boundary lines of societies and cultural regions, or that analyze interactions between peoples of different societies and cultural regions, or that examine the historical development and influence of large-scale, transregional systems or networks, or that otherwise offer global perspectives on the past. The chief point was that for purposes of the *JWH*, world history would mean approaches to the past that cross the national, cultural, geographical, ethnic, and other boundary lines that professional historians and other scholars conventionally observed. Often, of course, there are very good reasons to work within those boundary lines, and the founders of the *JWH* did not understand world history as a project that would displace all other forms of historical scholarship. Yet they recognized that recent scholarship had focused usefully on large-scale processes like mass migration, environmental change, biological exchange, cross-cultural trade, technological diffusion, imperial expansion, and the spread of religious and cultural traditions, all of which call for analytical frameworks larger than those conventionally adopted in historical scholarship. The plan was for *JWH* to serve as a forum for scholarship on these and other historical issues that require large-scale, transregional, continental, hemispheric, oceanic, or literally global frames of reference.

This point marked the crucial difference between the new *JWH* and an earlier historical journal published between 1953 and 1972 by UNESCO under the main title *Cahiers d'histoire mondiale*, with the subtitles *Journal of World History* and *Cuadernos de historia mundial*. The UNESCO journal presented first-rate scholarship, much of which had broad appeal. Yet *Cahiers d'histoire mondiale* was a journal of world history primarily in the sense that it would publish articles dealing with historical events that occurred in any part of the world. Some of its essays addressed larger comparative or systematic issues, including notably two seminal contributions by Marshall G. S. Hodgson.[6] Yet for all their high quality and inherent interest, most of the articles in the UNESCO journal focused on individual lands and threw light on the historical development of a single society, such as pharaonic Egypt, Renaissance Italy, colonial Mexico, or modern Japan.

Apart from the expectation that contributions would cross the usual national, cultural, geographical, and ethnic boundary lines in one way or another, the construction of world history adopted for the *JWH* was intentionally loose and open-ended. Founders of the *JWH* did not consider it appropriate to construe the field narrowly or to associate it specifically with any particular theoretical approach or school of thought, such as modernization analysis or world-system analysis. After all, at the time the *JWH* was under construction, world history was only just emerging as a field of professional historical interest—and indeed it continues to develop rapidly in several distinct directions at the present moment—so it did not seem useful to define world history so narrowly as to foreclose possibilities that the journal and the field of world history itself might move in directions that were not readily foreseeable in the late 1980s.

Actually Existing World History

Some quantitative data will be useful for purposes of characterizing more precisely the kinds of world history that the *JWH* has presented. The first seventeen volumes of the *JWH* (1990–2006) featured 195 articles (including review articles but excluding letters to the editor and brief book reviews). In three tables below I have indicated the principal chronological, geographical, and topical or thematic focus of these articles. Since I counted each article only once for each of the three tables, the tabulation is a little arbitrary: individual articles often deal with more than one chronological era, more than one geographical region, more than one topic or theme, and another observer might well sort some of the 195 articles into somewhat different categories. The arbitrariness of the sorting process is particularly prominent in the case of articles' geographical focus. In the nature of things, all *JWH* articles cross the conventional boundary lines in one way or another, but many of them still have strong resonance for a particular region. My tabulation below associates articles with the regions that strike me as their principal focus, but it also recognizes categories for contributions that explicitly take comparative, interregional, or global approaches. In any case, granting that the sorting of articles into chronological, geographical, and topical or thematic categories is imperfect, the three tables will serve at least as a rough guide to the scholarly understanding of world history that has emerged from the *JWH*.

Table 1. Chronological Focus of JWH Articles, 1990-2006

Ancient	Postclassical	Early Modern	Modern	Twentieth-Century	Other
3	14	44	50	45	39

While *JWH* articles have ranged from deep antiquity to the present, most have dealt with the early modern era (approximately 1500 to 1800), the modern era (approximately 1750 to 1900), and the twentieth century.

It is not surprising that most articles should deal with this half-millennium from 1500 to 2000, since most professional historians work in these eras for which relatively abundant documentation and source materials survive.

It is perhaps more surprising and certainly notable that a substantial minority of 39 articles (grouped here under the rubric "Other"), which amount to fully twenty percent of the total, deal with long stretches of time that involve two or more of these chronological categories. My sense is that very few professional historical journals routinely present large numbers of articles that deal with long stretches of time and explore historical experiences across the boundary lines of the conventionally recognized chronological eras. Although this was not one of the express or conscious intentions of the journal's founders, it is arguable that the forum created by the *JWH* has had the welcome side benefit of encouraging historians to think about their research in deeper chronological context than is commonly the case in professional historical scholarship.

A first glance at Table 1 might inspire disappointment that only a few articles deal with premodern times, including antiquity and the postclassical era. Indeed, it would be valuable for world historians to generate more scholarship on premodern times. It bears mention, however, that many of the 39 articles grouped under the rubric "Other" in fact pay substantial attention to premodern as well as modern times.

Table 2. Geographical Focus of JWH Articles, 1990-2006

Eastern Hemisphere	Oceania	Comparative and Interregional	World as a Whole		
3	8	44	34		
Americas	Africa	Eurasia	Europe		
21	9	7	12		
East Asia	South Asia	Southeast Asia	West Asia	Inner Eurasia	
20	15	6	10	6	

The geographical categories in Table 2 refer to somewhat incommensurate regions: they do not represent an ideal typology for world history or world geography but rather a reflection of the regions that have in fact served as the principal geographical focuses of *JWH* articles. From the data in Table 2 it is possible to infer that most *JWH* articles have crossed the conventionally observed national, geographical, and cultural boundary lines by way of exploring cases of cross-cultural interactions as they have played out in particular regions. As a result, it is reasonable to suggest that a given article contributes primarily to the understanding of East Asia, South Asia, Europe, or some other reasonably well defined region.

Table 2 presents two additional points, however, that strike me as particularly noteworthy. First, sizable numbers of articles have taken quite large regions as their geographical focus: the eastern hemisphere, Oceania, and inner Eurasia, for example. Just as the *JWH* has encouraged historians to adopt longer chronological frameworks than are common in professional historical scholarship, it has also pushed them to develop larger conceptions of social space for their analyses and to locate historical developments in larger geographical contexts. Second, a remarkable 78 out of 195 articles—a full forty percent—either undertake explicit comparisons between different world regions, or explore processes that work their effects across the boundary lines of different world regions, or make an effort to bring historical analysis and reasoning to the world as a whole. So far as I am aware, no other historical journal has presented such large numbers of articles that routinely trespass the geographical boundary lines that historians, area specialists, and other scholars typically recognize. Once again, then, it seems clear that the *JWH* has facilitated historians' efforts to conceive and develop new frameworks for historical analysis.

Table 3. Topical or Thematic Focus of JWH Articles, 1990-2006

Conceptual Issues	Methods and Theory	World Systems	Women's History and Gender History	Trade
41	18	3	5	8
Migrations	Environmental History	Political History	Economic History	Social History
8	11	15	10	9
Diplomacy and War	Imperialism and Colonialism	Religious History	Cultural History	Science and Technology
15	17	16	16	5

The main disappointment in the data of Table 3 is the low level of attention devoted to issues of women's history and gender history. Although they are by now universally recognized as fields of crucial significance, historians have persisted in conceiving issues of women's history and gender history almost exclusively within the frameworks of national communities. It would be extraordinarily enriching for the project of world history as well as for the projects of women's history and gender history for scholars in all these fields to engage in constructive and creative dialogue with one another—for world historians to draw on the insights of women's history and gender history in their comparative, cross-cultural, systematic, and global analyses, and also for women's historians and gender historians to venture beyond the confines of national communities and locate their own research in larger chronological, geographical, and cultural contexts.[7]

Excepting the cases of women's history and gender history, Table 3 suggests that the topics and themes of world historians' research, as reflected in *JWH* articles, are quite similar to those explored by the larger community of professional historians. *JWH* articles have dealt both with traditional staples of professional historical scholarship, such as political, social, and economic history, and with newer approaches, such as environmental, cultural, and migration history. It might seem peculiar that only three *JWH* articles appear in Table 3 under the rubric "World Systems," but it is worth pointing out that many articles represented under the rubrics "Trade," "Economic History," "Social History," and "Imperialism and Colonialism" reflect the influence of world-system scholarship. While world historians pay attention to world-systems studies as those studies have implications for the understanding of particular historical developments, it would be reasonable to infer that they part company with their colleagues in the other social sciences in that they shy away from reified constructs like "world system" (or "world-system," as some prefer) in favor of more flexible and historically sensitive categories.

Perhaps the most notable observation arising from Table 3 is the point that some 59 *JWH* articles, representing just over thirty percent of the total published between 1990 and 2006, deal with conceptual, methodological, and theoretical issues. This proportion is low in comparison with a journal like *History and Theory*, which has the specific mission of exploring conceptual, methodological, and theoretical issues. In comparison with most other professional historical journals, however, *JWH* has featured rather large numbers of articles on conceptual, methodological, and theoretical issues. Thus, while encouraging historians to frame their research in larger chronological and geographical contexts than is common in professional historical scholarship, the *JWH* has also provided opportunities for scholars to think afresh about the categories and approaches that are most useful for historical analysis, and particularly for analysis dealing with transregional and global developments rather than the experiences of national communities and individual societies.

As reflected in contributions to the *JWH*, world history is quite different from the nineteenth-century model of historical scholarship, which emphasized precise reconstruction of historical developments on the basis of documentary and preferably archival evidence. It is of course a widely recognized point that over the past generation or so, historical scholarship in general has increasingly represented a quest for historical meaning as well as a technical effort to reconstruct the past. Scholarship in world history clearly reflects this larger development. If anything, world history has emphasized the quest for historical meaning more than professional historical scholarship in general. By encouraging the adoption of longer chronological frameworks, the development of larger geographical constructs, and attention to conceptual, methodological, and theoretical issues, world history has encouraged scholars to understand specific historical experiences in larger relevant contexts, and indeed also to explore the nature and dimensions of those larger contexts themselves.

It is conceivable that this development carries with it a cost in the precision of historical knowledge. To the extent that historians today devote more attention to large chronological and geographical contexts, not to mention large conceptual, methodological, and theoretical issues, primary sources and historical evidence receive less attention, at least relatively, than they did in the work of earlier generations of historians. It might well be the case that historical scholarship of earlier generations focused so resolutely on primary sources that it sometimes overlooked the larger significance of historical thinking, and furthermore neglected to explore the problematic dimensions of historical scholarship itself. Yet even as historians today focus increased attention on questions of larger significance, they have a continuing obligation to base their work on the best available historical evidence. The task for all historians, including world historians and others as well, is to strike a balance between the interests of historical meaning and professional demands for historical precision.

Looking Ahead

The three tables presented above reflect the scholarship that has actually appeared in the first seventeen volumes of the *JWH*. There are at least two additional kinds of contributions that, as *JWH* editor, I have attempted to solicit for the journal, albeit with limited success. One kind of additional contribution that would be valuable for the *JWH* is the article offering direct engagement and debate between world historians and representatives of postmodern and postcolonial scholarship. Most world historians share with most postmodern and postcolonial scholars a strong desire to develop alternatives to Eurocentric historical constructions, but they take different approaches in doing so. World historians mostly seek to decenter Europe by locating it in larger transregional and global contexts and by viewing it as only one of many societies taking part in large-scale historical processes. By contrast, postmodern and postcolonial scholars generally disregard large-scale contexts and processes in favor of a focus on specific ethnic or racial identities. World historians fault postmodern and postcolonial scholars for ignoring important dimensions of historical reality, while postmodern and postcolonial scholars charge that large-scale approaches allow Eurocentrism to reenter historical scholarship by the back door. There is some cogency in all these points, and the tensions they generate could serve as the basis for fruitful discussion and debate. For the most part, however, world historians have preferred to express themselves in different forums from their postmodern and postcolonial colleagues, who for their own part have only rarely manifested any interest in addressing readers of the *JWH*.[8]

A second kind of contribution that would be valuable for the *JWH* is the essay offering analysis of the global past from perspectives other than those of the North American, western European, and Australasian scholars who have been most prominent among *JWH* authors. Most world historians, including *JWH* authors, strive conscientiously to avoid the traps of ethnocentrism, Eurocentrism, orientalism, and other snares that await scholars who venture beyond the historical experiences of their own societies to engage in comparative and cross-cultural analysis. Yet even the most careful, critical, and reflexive scholars inevitably reflect the influence of the unique combinations of values, interests, and experiences that shape their views and understandings of the world. Individual world historians will not necessarily adopt all the views of their colleagues in other societies, but world history as an intellectual project requires them to take other perspectives into account and engage in discussion, dialogue, and debate with colleagues who understand the global past in very different ways. One of the more useful goals for the *JWH* in future years will be to foster and facilitate the articulation of multiple perspectives on the global past.

From these last remarks it is clear that the *JWH* still has work to do. It has already performed welcome service, in my view, by providing a forum for comparative, cross-cultural, systematic, and otherwise global historical analysis. These approaches have usefully complemented more traditional historical scholarship, and they have advanced the development of world history as a field of basic research and historical analysis. If in years to come the *JWH* is able to promote discussion, dialogue, and debate between world historians from different world regions and provide a space for the articulation of multiple perspectives on the global past, it will serve not only to advance the cause of world history in particular but also to increase the value of professional historical scholarship in general.

Notes

1. For one example among many, see Micol Seigel, "World History's Narrative Problem," *Hispanic American Historical Review* 84 (2004): 431-446.
2. See the WHA constitution, published in the *World History Bulletin* 17:2 (Fall 2001): 17–18. The text is also accessible online at www.thewha.org/wha_constitution.php.
3. For a report on the meeting, see Craig A. Lockard, "Wingspread Conference," *World History Bulletin* 1:1 (Fall/Winter 1983): 7–9.
4. Craig A. Lockard, "The Promotion of Graduate Study and Research in World History," *World History Bulletin* 2:2 (Fall/Winter 1984): 6–7; Jerry H. Bentley, "Graduate Education and Research in World History," *World History Bulletin* 3:2 (Fall/Winter 1985–86): 9.
5. See Jerry H. Bentley, *Shapes of World History in Twentieth-Century Scholarship* (Washington, DC: American Historical Association, 1996), and "The New World History," in Lloyd Kramer and Sarah Maza, eds., *A Companion to Western Historical Thought* (Oxford: Blackwell, 2002), 393–416.
6. Marshall G. S. Hodgson, "The Hemispheric Interregional Approach to World History," *Cahiers d'histoire mondiale* 1 (1954): 17–23; and "The Unity of Later Islamic History," *Cahiers d'histoire mondiale* 5 (1960): 879–914.

7. Merry Wiesner-Hanks has called for comparative and cross-cultural approaches to women's history and gender history in several recent publications: *Christianity and Sexuality in the Early Modern World: Regulating Desire, Reforming Practice* (London: Routledge, 2000); *Gender in History* (Oxford: Blackwell, 2001); and "World History and the History of Women, Gender, and Sexuality," *Journal of World History* 18 (2007): 53–68.
8. For two efforts to explore some of these issues and encourage debate, see Jerry H. Bentley, "World History and Grand Narrative," in Benedikt Stuchtey and Eckhardt Fuchs, eds., *Writing World History, 1800-2000* (Oxford: Oxford University Press, 2003), 47-65; and "Myths, Wagers, and Some Moral Implications of World History," *Journal of World History* 16 (2005): 51-82.

CHAPTER 10

The Significance of the Research Institute for World History (NPO-IF) in Japan

Shingo Minamizuka

The institution called Research Institute for World History (RIWH) was founded in July 2004 in Tokyo. It is an independent institution, and does not belong to any universities, governmental organizations, or companies. It belongs to NPO–International Forum for Culture and History, a non-profit organization founded in 2000.[1] Its financial base is made up of contributions from individuals and organizations. The concrete purposes of the Institute are:

1. To promote interest in research and education on world history in Japan
2. To collect and provide information on research and education in world history
3. To popularize the necessity for study of world history in Japan
4. To maintain contact with other institutions and groups concerned with world history

We have only limited resources and manpower. We have no permanent researchers but have several casual researchers who are quite talented. We have excellent advisers: Professor Ivan T. Berend of UCLA; Masao Nishikawa, Professor Emeritus of Tokyo University; Yuichi Shimomura, Professor Emeritus of Chiba University; and Hiroshi Momose, Professor Emeritus of Tsuda College.[2]

The Background of RIWH

In order to explain the reasons for the initiation of the RIWH, I must briefly look back over the Japanese experience in world-historical writing. Japanese historiography has produced major achievements in the writing of world history. These achievements have been divided into two spheres. One is the history textbook for the junior high and high schools, while the other is the compilation of book series in world history. Since we already have several important works done by Prof. Masao Nishikawa and others concerning the history textbook problem,[3] I should like to introduce briefly the latter achievement—the compilation of book series in world history—which has not been introduced outside of Japan.

But before that, I should like to survey the process of introducing and formulating world history in Japan since the Meiji Era. In the 1870s and in the first half of 1880s we tried to develop such concepts of world history as "Bankokushi," meaning "history of all nations on earth." This introduced two trends of foreign endeavor for world history: one trend was to compose the world history as a collection of histories of individual countries with some histories of special topics (S. G. Goodrich's book was translated into Japanese beginning in 1876), while the other was to follow the development of the whole world, considering it as a large society or community on the earth (as was the case with E. A. Freeman's general history).[4] From the late 1880s the Japanese concept of world history became increasingly Euro-centric and white-centric, despising Asia, relying on William Swinton's book and others.[5] From the 1890s, however, Japanese world-historical writing insisted that Japan was as great as Europe and was to be the leader of Asian peoples.[6] It was in the beginning of the twentieth century that we introduced the term "world history"—it was, of course, characterized by Eurocentrism and Japan-centrism. This kind of world history could not prevent the Japanese invasion into Asia in the 1930s.

Compilation of series of world history started in the 1940s, at the initiative of several famous historians and the publishers. Since the end of World War II, we have had more than 20 series of books in world history. The first important world history that appeared in Japan was produced at the end of the 1940s under the editorship of the late Professors Namio Egami, Kentaro Murakawa, Noboru Niida, Shigeki Toyama, Bokuro Eguchi and Senroku Uehara. This was the *History of the World* in 6 volumes (published by

Mainichi Sinbun Publishing House, 1949–1954). This was the expression of our belief after the war that we had to live together with other peoples in the world. In the following years, there appeared seven series on world history in the 1960s, four in the 1970s, four in the 1980s, and nine in the 1990s.

One of the most important series on world history was the *Iwanami Course on World History* in 31 volumes (Iwanami Shoten Publishing House, 1969–71). This was the best achievement of world history in the 1960s. It is divided into ancient times, medieval times, modern times, and contemporary times, and each time period includes several volumes, with a "general view" and then follow-up articles on European and Asian (non-European) history. This is a collection of specialized articles on each given topic and many of the articles were of the highest standard for their time. It tried to place Japanese history in the perspective first of Asian and then Euro-American history, showing that we have to advance hand in hand with Asian people. It was also the best product of Japanese Marxist historians.

Although we did not have exciting series on world history in the 1970s, after the students' revolts in 1968–1969, in the 1980s there again appeared stimulating works. For example, *Visual History of the World* in 20 volumes (Kodansha Publishing House, 1984–89), *The New World History* in 12 volumes (University of Tokyo Press, 1986–89), and *Inquiries into World History* in 10 volumes (Iwanami Shoten Publishing House, 1989–91). Especially the second series tried to find new frontiers of researching and narrating world history through widening the perspective of individual historical studies. Some typical topics are the world of "untouchables," "traditional transformation," "individuals and communities," "common people's society," "identities of national minorities," and "modernization." The third series was a sincere amalgam of Marxist history and social history. It was not intended to describe world history but to investigate important methodological or individual topics in world history such as history and nature, technology, human movement (including migration), social association, discipline and integration, popular culture, authority and power, structuring the world, religion in history, and state and revolution.

After the collapse of socialist regimes in Russia and Eastern Europe, there has been chaos among historians in Japan too. The *Course on World History* in 12 volumes (University of Tokyo Press, 1995–96) and *World History Viewed from the "South"* in 6 volumes (Otsuki Shoten Publishing

House, 1999) are the Marxist effort to explain world history from a new perspective, though they are still not successful. Beside these works there appeared more "positivist" series, which are represented by *World History* in 30 volumes (Chuokoronsha Publishing House, 1996–99), and *New Iwanami Course on World History* in 29 volumes (Iwanami Shoten Publishing House, 1997–2000). Meanwhile, *World History Seen from Regions* in 12 volumes (Yamakawa Shuppansha Publishing House, 1997–2000) is an ambitious experiment in composing world history from the viewpoint of regions. It is a series of volumes dealing with various themes on regional history—defining a region, images of regions, formation of regions, regional history of ecology, human movement, time, belief, living, market, and domination.

After reflection on the whole experience of world history in Japan, one can easily see that although there have been interesting efforts to conceptualize world history in Japan, the main characteristics are that these were the mixture of the two trends of the Meiji Era. There is no world history that is written from a consistent point of view or consistent method.

Why is the RIWH necessary?

Is it a world history if a series covers the whole of the national or regional histories on the earth? Our Institute tries to pursue the missing link. The purpose of the Institute is thus to find the possibilities for searching out viewpoints or methods for building world history beyond the terms of collections of national (or regional) histories on the earth.

We have developed many detailed and specialized histories in these several decades, but we have lost long-term and comprehensive perspective of the world where we live. Every historian believes that, if he/she produces a high-standard achievement in his/her special field, it will contribute to enriching world history, or someone will make use of it to produce world history. The separated, subdivided situation of historical sciences that has advanced since the 1980s has proved not only to be weak in the face of "globalization" but to be an obstacle to forming a grand-scale perspective, by reducing historical studies to detailed and specialized or even "hobby-like" works.

Although there were quite a lot of series on world history published in Japan, and though some of them seriously tried to conceptualize world history, it cannot be denied that the series were mainly collections of individual works; the effort to form world history was only sporadic.

Possibilities of World History

So far we, historians of the world, have found several possibilities as to the method of constructing world history. The most important achievement in overcoming national histories was comparative economic history, but the fact is that the national economic histories are not connected to each other by mere comparison. We have no economic history of the world yet. The civilizational approach is another traditional one: it has revived recently in the face of the rise of Islamic power. Mega-regional historical studies such as the history of the Indian Ocean, pan-Atlantic history, Eurasian history, and others are emerging as important approaches to world history. World history of particular themes such as the history of tea, coffee, environment, and gender is also gaining importance. History of the movements of human beings, including migration across the earth, may also create a powerful drive to world history. History of the philosophy of world history going back to the period of the Enlightenment, though important, has to be developed to include Asian philosophy too. And the world-system approach is also promising, though it tends to be static and should be reviewed from the viewpoint of Asia. Lastly, history of international relations, which is a rather traditional approach, is developing a new outlook including more historical method.

Although each has some limitations itself, as we have seen, these approaches seem to be promising. But I wonder what kind of viewpoint we should adopt in using these approaches. Is it possible to constitute a world history that all the people can accept? Or will we have several world histories? We think that we will have plural world histories for the time being or even longer. As a result, our point is that, since world history from the fifteenth century to the middle of the nineteenth century was one where the "North" subjugated the "South," world history "from below" should be one of the most important versions, if we are to refrain from being "European-oriented."

In this sense, our guiding figure for considering world history is the late Professor Bokuro Eguchi (Tokyo University). As a specialist on the age of imperialism, he left many suggestions for world history. According to him, "comparison" must lead to "relation." If a certain part of the world was "backward," it was so because there was an "advanced" part at its side. The "advanced" part stands in the way of the "backward." And the "advanced" part makes use of the "backward" factors within its own region too. We have to think of a world where every part of the globe is connected to each other in one sense or another. Thus if there is a relaxation of conflict between powers in one part of the world, there must be an increase of tension in another part of the world.

As a historian of the age of imperialism, Eguchi did not consider the world as a world made of nation states but as a holistic imperial power confronting the whole people in Asia and Africa, though there were mutual conflicts among the Powers. He also emphasized the limitation of our recognition of the facts. Looking at things from the "North"—that is, developed countries—it is easy to make mistakes even though it may seem highly sophisticated, while the viewpoint of the "South"—that is underdeveloped countries—does not easily lead to mistakes, however unsophisticated and instinctive it may seem. It is like the saying in the Bible that it is more difficult for the rich to get to the Promised Land than for a camel to go through the eye of a needle. Thus he taught us to see the world always from the "South."

Activities of RIWH

Following the purposes of our Institute listed above, we are organizing discussion meetings on the method of world history, introducing global achievements of world history including translation and review of important works, examining the achievements of world history in Japan, including the works of the late Professor Bokuro Eguchi, and organizing our "world history caravans."

Introduction to Foreign Achievements in World History. We have organized several discussion meeting on the possibilities of world history, with Professor Patrick Manning (U.S.), Professor Ivan T. Berend (U.S.), Dr. Erzsebet Szalai (Hungary), Dr. Francisco Zapata (Mexico), and Dr. Tha Thi Thuy (Vietnam) as our guests. Through these discussions we have learned that our project for world history is not an isolated movement, and that we had better present the Japanese achievements to the world more explicitly. World historians elsewhere are pondering the same possibilities of constituting world history, and we have to pay attention to their point of view when we try to formulate world history.

We are trying to introduce recent major works on world history. We are now undertaking the translation of P. Manning, *Navigating World History: Historians Create a Global Past* (Palgrave Macmillan, 2003) into Japanese. We have also reviewed important books and articles on world history such as A. G. Hopkins, ed., *Globalization and World History* (Pimlico, 2002), and Hanna Schissler and Yasemin Nuhoğlu Soysal, eds., *The Nation, Europe, and the World* (Berghahn Books, 2005). We are introducing to our members important website information that is useful for following the newest trends of research and education in world history.

Examination of the Japanese achievements in world history. We have found it important to examine the Japanese achievements in world history after World War II in order to communicate with world historians abroad. First, we started to examine the works by Professor Eguchi, as already mentioned, and we are planning to translate his main works into English and to put them on our web site. Secondly, we have reviewed the series of world history published in Japan since the end of the war, some part of which is introduced above. The complete presentation is to be found in our website.

Thirdly, we are dealing with the problems of the textbook of world history. We discussed the problems of the *New History Textbook* for the junior high schools, published by the ultra-nationalists, from the viewpoint of world history. Critique of the *New History Textbook* is written by myself and can be seen on our website.[7] The essential characteristics of *New History Textbook* are as follows. The Emperor (Tennno) system is the pillar of Japanese history. The *New History Textbook* emphasizes the unbroken line of emperors starting from Jinmu Tenno, though Jinmu was a legendary person. The Tenno is argued to have been behind the *bushi* (samurai, warrior) power since the twelfth century. The Meiji Restoration of 1868 is interpreted as the product of those bushis who were loyal to Tenno; the Second World War, it is argued, was also ended by the decision of Tenno. There is no mention of the responsibility of Tenno for the beginning and prolonging of the war: Japan was and is a peaceful nation which lives comfortably around the Tenno. Thus the general argument is that the Western powers always wanted to invade Asia, from the sixteenth century (the age of Columbus), and it was

Japan who resisted and tried to expel them from Asia—with World War II (the Great East-Asian War) being another case. It is difficult for the world to accept these interpretations.

At the same time, we are trying to translate into English a typical history textbook for junior high school to show how world history has traditionally been intertwined into the context of Japanese history. The recent *New History Textbook* is a complete reaction to this "tradition" by cutting world history off from Japanese history, distorting the context of world history in such a way as to argue that the foreign powers were always threatening Japan.

Constructing World history

RIHW is ambitiously trying to construct world history in a positive way. We are engaged in the study of two periods.

1890–1905. We are trying to construct cross-regional world history covering the period of from 1890 to 1905—that is, the period of the Sino-Japanese war and the Russo-Japanese war. Our method is double. On the one hand we make much of the economic, social and cultural history of imperialism; on the other hand we use the history of cross-regional international relations with local history in mind. In this case we see history not from the viewpoint of the powers but from the viewpoint of Asia and Africa, trying to place the ideas and movements of native resistance into a broad perspective. More concretely;

1. With the Russo-French Alliance (1891–1894), the balance of power within Europe was thought to have been established; any further conflict in Europe was expected to lead to war in Europe.
2. Due to the Korean problem caused by peasant revolt, the Sino-Japanese War occurred in 1894–1895, resulting in the loss of the war by China, which led to the penetration of western powers into China.
3. This gave rise to the Boxer Rising, which was indigenous but anti-imperialist. Japan in turn started to become a Power, but its rise was prevented by the Triple Intervention (by Russia, France and Germany), leading to increased nationalism in Japan.
4. Japan concluded an Anglo-Japanese Alliance in 1902. The UK was greatly occupied with the Boer War which (though it began after British detente with France following the Fashoda confrontation in 1898) met with resistance not only from the Boers but also indigenous people.

5. The penetration of western Powers into the Far East caused a conflict between Russia and Japan, which led to the Russo-Japanese War, 1904–1905. It was actually not just a war between Russia and Japan but also between France and Germany (who supported Russia) on one hand and the UK and the U.S. (who were on Japan's side) on the other. So the war had to be ended before either of the rival Powers was beaten completely.
6. The Russo-Japanese War signified that a balance of power in the Far East was thought to have been reached. While the possible conflicts among Japan, Russia, and the U.S. were covered by "pacts," the main contradiction of imperialism shifted to Africa and the Middle East: to Moroccan incidents involving Germany, Italian ambition in Africa, and the Persian Revolution.
7. No sooner had these crises been settled than a serious crisis arose from the Austrian annexation of Bosnia-Herzegovina in 1908, which caused local resistance and finally led to the First World War.

Thus, though the story is rather complicated, we want to see world history from the viewpoint of cross-regional history using international relations and local development.

The "long 1980s." We are trying to construct cross-regional world history of the "long 1980s" from the same point of view. The "9/11" terrorism was the product of the history of at least the previous decade, that is, the 1990s. What were the characteristics of the 1990s? First, U.S. monocentric rule became possible after the collapse of the USSR in 1991. Secondly, the U.S. military commitment to the Middle East escalated after the Gulf War of 1990, especially in that the U.S. military presence in Saudi Arabia was expanded and strengthened. Thirdly, the Islamic extreme fundamentalists were encouraged and they directed their energies against U.S. policy. These considerations lead us to the question of why such significant events occurred in 1990–1991. This is what we are researching now. In our opinion, the 1980s had begun already in 1979 and ended in 1991. So we had better label the period as the "long 1980s."

1. By the end of the 1970s, socialist regimes in Africa and Latin America had been forced to collapse as a result of the Cold War. On the Eurasian continent, however, socialist regimes kept enough vitality,

except in the USSR, Eastern Europe, and China. The U.S. was driven out of Vietnam and North and South Vietnam were united under socialist initiative. Afghanistan was coming under socialist influence, while Iraq was still under socialist influence.

2. In 1979, however, there occurred three important events that threatened the socialist regimes in Eurasia: the Iranian Revolution (February 1979), the Sino-Vietnamese War (February-March 1979), and the Soviet invasion of Afghanistan (December 1979). These marked the beginning of the "long 1980s." These three elements worked toward the collapse of the "Soviet Empire" and the direct confrontation of Islam and Israel.

3. Here two directions developed. The three factors mentioned above had a negative impact upon the Soviet Empire in addition to the economic and budgetary crisis owing to the military burden since the 1970s under the "Cold War." These provided the background for Gorbachev's *perestroika*, which began in 1985. Perestroika, in turn, was one of the important factors in the collapse of socialism in East Central Europe in 1989, though it was only one factor among several reasons for the collapse. Though there were many factors concerning the collapse of socialism in Eastern Europe, the decisive one was the economic weakness of USSR, which made it impossible for the USSR to support East Central Europe and other countries belonging to the Soviet Empire. And the collapse of socialism in East Central Europe and the Baltic as well as the independence movements of the Caucasian and Middle Asia led to the collapse of the USSR itself in 1991.

4. On the other hand, the Iranian Revolution had several effects on the international scene that would finally lead to the Gulf War. These included conflict with Iraq that led to the Iran-Iraq War, stimulation of the Lebanese struggle against Israel, prolongation of the Soviet military invasion in Afghanistan, and the growing U.S. military presence. The Iran-Iraq War (1980–1988) occurred under the direct influence of the Iranian Revolution. It was important that the USSR, the West, and Arab states supported Iraq for fear of the expansion of the Iranian Revolution: this foreign support strengthened Saddam Hussein's regime during the war. Under his rule the national-socialist regime of the Baath party was transformed

into mere one-party domination. It is important to pay attention to the Lebanese problem, which became more complicated due to the influence of the Iranian Revolution. Through the Shi'a Muslim movements in Lebanon the Iranian Revolution became connected with the Israel-Palestine problem.

5. The Gulf War (August 1990–February 1991) was the result of the accumulated factors of international relations in the Middle East during the "long 1980s." Although many reasons are listed as the cause of the war, the most important factor was the changed character of the Saddam Hussein regime that was supported by the foreign powers during the Iran-Iraq War. And the important international consequences of that war were: Shi'a Muslim movements from Iran (through Iraq and Syria) to Lebanon becoming involved in the Palestine problems and facing Israel; almost complete withdrawal of the USSR from the Middle East; and strengthened U.S. military and political presence in the Middle East, especially in Saudi Arabia. Thus, monolithic rule by the U.S. took form in the Middle East, against which Arab and Islamic protest increased, resulting in the expansion of terrorism.

The above discussion shows the close relationships in the history of the regions of the world and shows how the events in 1989–1991 were the result of the global development of the "long 1980s."

But these events should be considered against the more structural background that distinguishes the "long 1980s" from the previous period. The previous period, the 1970s, provided the historical stage that was characterized by the beginning of "globalization." This globalization was made possible by the rapid advance of communication and information technology and realized by economic and financial transformation on the international scene. And it was promoted by the new ideology, neo-liberalism, which advocated the so-called "Structural Adjustment Policy" (SAP) and believed in "civil society." The U.S. was able to take advantage of this process of globalization, while the socialist states failed to catch up with it in the "long 1980s." The "South" (the developing countries) was almost the victim of the process.

Although this interpretation is still a hypothesis, we are trying, in our analysis, to construct world history from double approaches. On the one hand we make much of the economic, social, and cultural history of the "long 1980s," the age of globalization. On the other hand we use the history of cross-regional international relations with local history in mind.

Popularizing World History: "World History Caravan"

For popularizing the understanding of world history we are organizing "world history caravans," which are intended to organize talks with local people in the countryside on world history and the relationship of local history to large-scale world history. We have been to Yamato City in Niigata Prefecture, and to Matsumoto City, Iida City, and Nagiso Town, all in Nagano Prefecture. Participants are teachers of history in the local junior high schools and high schools, as well as students, housewives, pensioners, businessmen, local publishers, and newspaper writers.

Topics so far have included the cross-regional history of the world in the period of the Sino-Japanese War and Russo-Japanese War and the cross-regional history of the world before the First World War. The RIWH presented an image of the grand history of the given period and the local historians did the detailed history of the local society in the given period. We present world history from a double approach: a structural approach and cross-regional international relations with local history in mind.

Further, we are trying one more, much more interesting experiment in constructing world history. We are trying to describe the world history of 1890–1905 through following the movement and experiences of a group of Japanese traveling as a drama troupe including a famous geisha, Sadayakko. They traveled all over the U.S. and Europe within a few years, and were faced with many problems and delights. Their history serves a very interesting introduction into imaging world history.

Happily, we found unexpected relations of local history with grand history. These surprises made the people who participated feel the importance of thinking about history at a world scale.

THE SIGNIFICANCE OF THE RESEARCH INSTITUTE FOR WORLD HISTORY

Notes

1. The institute's website is at www.npo-if.jp/riwh/index.html. "NPO" refers to "non-profit organization."
2. In addition, the late Mr. Kazuo Tanaka, a distinguished Balkanist, served as an advisor.
3. As for the history textbook problems in Japan, see Kazuhiko Kimijima, "Rekishikyouiku to Kyoukasho-mondai [History Teaching and the History Textbook Problem]," in Rekishigaku Kenkyukai ed.., *Historical Studies in Japan 1980–2000: Trends and Perspectives* (Tokyo: Aoki Publishing House, 2002); Hikakushi-Hikakurekisihikyouiku Kenkyuukai, ed., *Jikokushi to Sekaisi [History of Our Own Country and World History]* (Tokyo: Miraisha Publishing House, 1985); Rekishigaku Kenkyukai, ed., *Rekishikenkyu no Genzai to Kyoukasho Mondai [Present Situation of Historical Studies and the History Textbook Problem]* (Tokyo, 2005); and Masao Nishikawa, "Convenor's Overview" for the session on "Textbooks: From the Narrative of the Nation to the Narrative of Citizens," *Twentieth International Congress of Historical Sciences: Programme* (Sydney, 2005),183–186.
4. We have several Japanese translations of Samuel. G. Goodrich, *Peter Parley's Universal History, on the Basis of Geography* (New York: Ivison, Phinney, Blakeman, 1869), as follows: *Bankokushi*, trans. Kouhei Makiyama, 2 vols. (1876); *Bankokushi-tyokuyaku*, trans. Taki Kimura (1887); *Bankokushi-tyokuyaku*, trans. Haruaki Fujita, 2 vols. (1887); *Bankokushi-tyokuyaku*, trans. Einosuke Nakao, (1888); and others.
    Edward A.Freeman's book, *General Sketch of History* (New York: H. Holt and Co., 1874), has only one translation: *Bankokushiyou*, trans. Shigeo Sekifuji, 12 vols. (1888).
5. We have also several translations of William Swinton, *Outlines of the World's History* (New York: Ivison, Blakeman, Taylor, and Co., 1874): *Bankokushi-tyokuyaku*, trans. Yoshiyuki Nishiyama, (1885); *Bankokushi*, trans. Sakae Ueda (1886); *Bankokushi-tyokuyaku*, trans. Tadao Kurino, 2 vols. (1887); and others.
6. Matsumoto Michitaka, "Meijikini okeru kokuminno taigaikanno ikusei—bankokushi kyoukashono bunsekiwo toosite [On the education of outward perspective of the nation in the Meiji Era—Through the analysis of bankokushi textbooks]," in H. Masutani and S. Ito, eds., *Ekkyousuru bunka to kokumintougou [Borderless Culture and National Integration]* (Tokyo: Tokyo University Press, 1998), 185–203.
7. www.npo-if.jp/riwh/index.html.

CHAPTER 11

Museums and World History

Leslie Witz[1]

It is instructive to do an internet search using the key words "museums, world, and history." Heading the results list of 190,000,000 finds, and the only institution which specifically designates itself as a general museum of world history, is the Berman Museum in Anniston, Alabama, which claims it has "over 3,000 objects related to world history in five galleries." The impression from the internet search is that world history in this museum is a somewhat arbitrary assemblage of artefacts (with an emphasis on weaponry and works of fine art) from a range of settings (many from Germany at the end of World War II), collected by Colonel Farley Berman and his wife Germaine.[2] Interestingly, in positions two and four on the list of search results are the Natural History Museum in London and the American Museum of Natural History, respectively. They are not placed on the list as museums of world history, but they market themselves as topping a research and educational hierarchy labeled "the world" of natural history museums.[3] I want to argue though that they, and many other museums, are both locations of and for world history.

Underlying this argument is the notion of the museum that Stuart Hall has presented:

> A museum does not deal solely with *objects*, but more importantly, with ... *ideas*—notions of what the world is or should be. Museums do not simply issue objective descriptions or form logical assemblages; they generate representations and attribute value and meaning in line with certain perspectives

155

or classificatory schemas which are historically specific. They do not so much reflect the world through objects as use them to mobilise representations of the world past and present.[4]

In this characterization of museums and their functions, Hall is using the term "world" neither to denote global linkages nor as an ever-expanding incorporative spatial domain. Instead the "world" is a site of appropriation and association, and the museum is one setting where its meanings are generated, transmitted, altered, and contested.

Utilizing this concept of museums as institutions of representation opens up productive possibilities for world historians. There is, of course, the contextual possibility, where world history becomes a backdrop to situate the emergence and development of museums as institutions that create a nationalized public citizenry.[5] Aligned to this is the investigation of how museum collections were created, sustained, and classified in global networks of power and control, such as imperial conquest.[6] This would be the type of historical specificity demanded in Hall's notion of the museum.

But if, as Hall argues further, museums are in themselves mobilizing agents that construct the world, a further set of issues emerges for historians around the representations of the world and its histories that come to be displayed. Barbara Kirshenblatt-Gimblett has argued that museums can be characterized, in several ways, as "surrogates for travel."[7] Not only have the objects in collections and displays traveled, often on circuitous and complex routes, on their way to the museum, but museums also create environments to encounter disparate localities and their histories. These are situated within the classificatory maps that direct visitors and link an interior world, presented as reflections of reality, but which are in effect "contingent"—"devices [that] . . . serve to signify certain kinds of cultural practice."[8] This often takes its most elaborate form in the large natural history museums where the collection, classification, and display of humans and/in nature reproduces and legitimizes ideas about society. The collections, classification, and displays of indigenous peoples in natural history museums, for instance, were often based upon racialized notions of society that had their origins in colonial encounters and the pursuit of research in the field of physical anthropology.[9]

The classificatory and exhibitionary strategies employed therefore challenge historians to analyze how and why ideas about the world are conceptualized in the museum, the histories of those notions, and how world history is represented. I want to pursue some of these challenges in relation to two museums, a maritime museum in South Africa and an ethnographic museum in the Netherlands, both of which are explicitly concerned with representing spatial and temporal linkages and associations across diverse regions.

An Event in World History

Maritime museums are perhaps the easiest form of museum to associate with the category of world history. They are explicitly about linkages in the past between different parts of the globe. Histories constructed on the foundations of the biography of the captain/explorer/traveler often provide the means to develop temporal and spatial narratives of departures and arrivals, where world history becomes cast in a series of unique and originary moments. Through their artifacts and displays that reify the technologies and instruments of maritime travel, they also present moments of first meeting or arrival, initially as encounters with "otherness," but increasingly as multicultural contact. In this manner the event of world history is constituted, not simply by that which happened, but in its "formation, regulation and transformation"[10] in the museum.

The Maritime Museum at the Bartolomeu Dias Museum complex in the Western Cape town of Mossel Bay employs such a strategy. The largest building on the campus is one that celebrates and pays homage to the rounding of the Cape of Good Hope by the Portuguese captain, Bartolomeu Dias, in 1488. Artefacts, photographs and ephemera produced for and derived from a quincentenary festival of this moment give this institution its claims to permanence and authenticity as a museum. An extensive photographic collection, containing many of the images from the festival proceedings, adorns the walls of one of the museum's galleries. Complementing the photographs are artifacts from the festival: commemorative coins that were struck for the occasion, the costumes worn by the participants in the pageantry, and a small-scale model of a caravel made of icing sugar. But undoubtedly the highlight for visitors, and the primary reason for the museum's popularity, is the presence of a reconstructed caravel that sailed from Portugal to Mossel Bay at the end of 1987. The opportunity to go on board, walk around the deck, stand beneath the masts, and then to descend to view the sleeping quarters on what is presented as a full-scale model of a fifteenth-century caravel that looks "exactly like its predecessor" from the outside entices the visitor. Although the ship is stationary, and a notice does tell visitors that the replica differed from the original in that it had "luxuries" for the crew, an engine and modern navigational equipment, visitors to the museum imagine themselves at sea in a fifteenth- (and not a twentieth-) century historical drama.

For the world historian, much of what is represented in the Bartolomeu Dias museum must seem, at best, archaic. Its celebration of the maritime as personified through the "discoverer" speaks to a commemorative type of world history based upon a teleological narrative of western progress. For the world historian, the straightforward role is to act as verifier and authenticator, to facilitate corrective and alternative interpretations. When a dilemma label alerts visitors that, "the Bartolomeu Dias Museum Complex is aware of a number of grammatical and historical errors in the text" in one of its exhibitions, such a methodology seems entirely appropriate. Yet, what this type of historical approach does is to regard history primarily as text. Exhibitions, using visual codes and museological conventions, are much more than manifestations of an historian's script. The key question for the world historian (as it is for those who are trying to transform this museum in post-apartheid South Africa) is: how does one analyze the museum's signifier, and its most popular exhibit—the caravel—and, following that, what are the implications for its display?

Addressing this question requires thinking about what Bennett calls a past-present-future alignment, where histories are created within a contemporary scenario and are projected into the future along a trajectory in "a never-ending story of development."[11] Very briefly, the Dias museum and the carvel project speak to a coming together of post-revolutionary Portuguese and late-apartheid South African public national pasts to create an event in world history at the end of the twentieth century.

Explicitly, the commemorations of the "discoveries" in Portugal, which began with the Dias festival in 1988 and the construction of the caravel, were seen to compensate for the end of the Portuguese imperial project. The end of dictatorship in Portugal in 1974 had been followed by the collapse of the Portuguese empire in Guiné-Bissau, Mozambique and Angola, a counter-coup in Portugal, and the assumption of a semblance of a democratic form of government under the military that lasted until 1986. When the army ceded control, the socialist Mario Soares was elected president and the conservative Cavaco Silva became prime minister.[12] Wanting to assert Portugal as a modern European nation that was entering the European Economic Community, in January 1987 Silva's government set up a National Board for the Celebration of the Portuguese Discoveries and proclaimed that the Portuguese explorers should become examples of national progress, to "revive national pride, and to remember the contribution we made to the improved knowledge of Man and the Universe."[13] In a moment of ardent nationalist fervor, Commander Rodrigues da Costa, a member of the National Board maintained that "from 1480 to 1520, we were the greatest in the world, no doubt about it." "We have lost our empire; now we must discover ourselves," said da Costa.[14]

In South Africa the organizers of the Dias festival asserted a multiculturalism that was within the bounds of (but attempting to be distinct from) the apartheid state. This was in accord with the attempts to reform and reconstitute apartheid in the 1980s, where repressive mechanisms were set in place accompanied by attempts to bring different groupings of people into the system through carefully selected and appointed "black" representatives. With the National Party government proclaiming that it was reforming apartheid, the land was depicted in festival narratives as already inhabited prior to Dias's arrival. The caravel project also enabled the South African government to assert itself as part of the world, attempting to confront the international boycott of apartheid South Africa that was becoming more effective in the 1980s. By turning the festival and the voyage of the caravel into a commemoration of a "great event in world history" the organizers claimed that what was being celebrated was the "wonderful discovery" of the sea route to India, a breakthrough that was ranked "as equal to modern space travel."[15]

This example enables world historians to analyze museum displays and collections as productions of history. Here the festival, on which the museum is founded, provides an opportunity to think through the workings of global systems and how they produce pasts. Imperial networks, their collapse, the formation of associations of political and economic integration, and the effects of international solidarity movements all contributed to the form that the Bartolomeu Dias museum takes today. For historians, museums are a way of considering how the contemporary "world" produces the interior world of association in the museum. In the museum itself, the challenge is how to make that process visible, to display the caravel, not as a replica of Dias's ship, but as a creation in the nexus of national and international politics in the late twentieth century.

Eastward Bound! (Oostwaarts!): **A History of Colonial Collecting**

One museum that has attempted to make "the history of its collection and display ... visible"[16] is the Koninklijk Instituut voor de Tropen (KIT) Tropenmuseum (Museum of the Royal Tropical Institute) in Amsterdam. The Tropenmuseum can be broadly categorized as an ethnographic museum, an institution which features "objects as the 'material culture' of peoples who have been considered, since the mid-nineteenth century, to have been the appropriate target of anthropological research."[17] For the world historian to track and analyze changes at the Tropenmusem, since it started in Harleem in 1871 as the Colonial Museum, is not only to situate the museum within Dutch colonial encounters and their aftermath but also to see how the world was shaped and re-shaped within the museum.

The initial collection of the Colonial Museum consisted mostly of products of the Dutch colonial world in the East Indies, including a section on "native objects and crafts." In 1926 the museum was moved and subsumed into the work of the Colonial Institute in Amsterdam, the "bulwark of colonial knowledge" in the Netherlands.[18] The Institute gave the museum a large exhibition space with two distinct components, colonial trade and ethnology.[19] The latter incorporated a substantial collection from the Amsterdam zoo (Artis), which included "very good pieces from Africa, China, Korea, and Japan."[20] After the Second World War the Dutch started to lose control of their colonies in the East Indies, and the Institute could no longer present itself as the center for collection and research for Dutch colonial possessions. In an attempt to establish an alignment with these new political trends, the Colonial Institute became the Indisch Instituut, with a similar name change to the museum section. A few years later, when a new Indonesian nation emerged, the name was again altered to reflect a broader focus on collecting, researching and exhibiting the "Third World" in Africa, Asia, Latin America, and the Caribbean. In 1950 the Tropical Museum (*Tropenmuseum*) of the Royal Tropical Institute (KIT) was formally constituted.[21]

By the 1970s, former colonizing powers were increasingly seeking to establish development relationships with ex-colonies that were to be based upon notions of people, not as inferior, but as equals with "their own histories and cultures."[22] This was articulated in the Netherlands under the title of "development cooperation." An association between the collection and representation of the existing culture of Third World countries and successive Dutch governments' policies of providing development aid was designed to form the basis of much more amenable cooperative arrangements.

In the schema of "development cooperation," the role envisaged for the KIT was to carry out research on "up-to-date development practices in the agricultural and health sectors." The function of the museum would be to become a "presentation center for the Third World in which the Dutch public could learn about the tropics and the Netherlands' relationship with these."[23] No longer was the colonial official or the ethnologist the source of the museum's collections. The development officer had replaced them.[24] Colonial collections were placed in storage. History, particularly that associated with the Dutch colonial period, "vanished from the museum." New exhibitions, making extensive use of text and photographs, presented contemporary life in the tropics, how problems were emerging and the possibility of developmental solutions that could emerge through international cooperation. Re-created scenes of urban and rural life replaced history, with the emphasis placed on cultural diversity, more often than not represented by an "ordinary" family unit, sited in an archetypal household, as the basis of development.[25] Amongst these were displays, in the West Asia and North Africa sections on the second floor of the museum, of the interior of a house in the Swat valley in Pakistan filled with personal artifacts, a nomad tent of the Central steppes, and a room showing the life of a family in Marrakesh.

At the end of the twentieth and the beginning of the twenty-first century, museums in the Netherlands embarked upon elaborate plans to reconstitute themselves, to re-position and market themselves as global institutions. National museums were turned into private foundations, new buildings were constructed, major renovations undertaken, and taxonomic categories of collection and exhibition were reconceptualized. One major shift was that museums became primarily institutions of display—major architectural firms were called in to re-design and refurbish interiors. At the National Museum of Ethnology in Leiden and the Ethnology Museum in Rotterdam (re-named the World Museum), the aesthetics of presentation became paramount. This aestheticization of culture is presented as challenging the classificatory division between the art and the ethnographic museum. This division refers to an "art-culture" system, where in an art museum the item on display is commonly identified as a work with a particular artist and remarked upon for its beauty and originality. In a space defined as ethnographic the item is classified by its cultural associations and placed together with similar objects in order to generate information, interest and, more latterly, understanding.[26] Through the refurbishment and reconstitution of museums of ethnology, it is claimed that the objects have journeyed into the category of art.[27] Yet, despite these assertions, the museums of ethnology, in both Leiden and Rotterdam, utilize regional categories that are often derived from the colonial divisions and locate objects in the museums as representative of this regional culture (although there are examples included of cultural interaction). Moreover the visit to the National Museum of Ethnology in Leiden is marketed as a "voyage of discovery" to "distant and unfamiliar places"[28], almost inadvertently rehearsing the tropes of colonial conquest and an "anthropology of primitivism"[29] that it claims to be working against.

The Tropenmuseum in Amsterdam has embarked upon a route very different route from the ones taken by the museums of ethnology in Rotterdam and Leiden. The changes at the Tropen were driven by practical considerations: a desire to change from a pastiche to a more coherent exhibitionary arrangement and a political commitment to becoming an "inclusive multicultural museum." The latter entailed a radical re-thinking of the relationship between audiences and the displays in the museum.

> We have to answer the question: whose cultural heritage is it we keep in our stores, who are the experts and for whom do we display it? We do not want to lose our traditional Dutch visitors, rooted in Dutch culture, who have grown up with the images and views that the museum produced. And we want to win the new Dutchmen with a non-western background who have an uneasy relationship with this essentializing tradition and not easily feel at home in a museum of which they know that it used to inform about them without really involving them.[30]

This introspection informed the decision to reconceptualize the first floor of the museum into an exhibition space that dealt broadly with the theme of Dutch colonialism. In this framework, multiculturalism did not mean the display of other cultures, as had been the strategy in both the colonial and development cooperation phases of the museum. Instead, interrogating the workings of various layers of Dutch society in the Netherlands and in the East Indies, "historicizing the Tropenmuseum collections" and incorporating the existing colonial building into the new reflexive exhibitionary structure became key elements in the strategy "to turn the museum into an inclusive multicultural institution within Dutch society."[31]

The first phase of this radical reorientation away from development cooperation towards displaying the colonial past was with the exhibition *Eastward Bound! (Oostwaarts!): Art, culture and colonialism*. *Oostwaarts!*, like the exhibitions at the museums of ethnology in Rotterdam and Leiden, also placed a great deal of emphasis on the aesthetic nature of displaying their collections. But it went much further than "beauty placed behind glasses"[32] by focusing on the colonial culture, the collectors of culture, their modes of appropriation and the relations of colonial power that dominated almost all spheres of political and social life in the Dutch East Indies. How Dutchness was created in the colonial encounter was a key part of the exhibition:

> In our exhibition we demonstrate that the concept of Dutch citizenship, about which so much is being said nowadays within the context of the integration policy, in the first instance was formed in the colonial context. It was overseas in the East Indies, in relation to the culture that surrounded them, that Dutch people started to feel Dutch; as people who did not belong to one or other ideological group, but who did belong to a nation that encompassed all these ideological or religious groups. Their contentment and their discontentment about their lot in Indonesian society was an integral part of that concept.[33]

A central part of the exhibition was the casts of archetypal colonial characters in cylindrical time capsules. These casts of colonial figures—such as the administrator, the soldier, and the missionary—not only narrated their stories but also were intended as a reflection upon the use of casts of indigenous people in ethnology museums.³⁴ The exhibitionary strategy on the first floor balcony signaled that the Tropenmuseum was no longer primarily considering itself as a "window on the south." Instead, what it means to be Dutch in the contemporary multicultural Netherlands was now the first item on the agenda.³⁵

These shifts in the collecting and exhibitionary strategies at the Tropenmuseum can provide the starting point for an historical examination of the role of museum in constituting and reconstituting nationalized citizenries through the circuits of international networks of power and control. From a colonial museum in the late nineteenth century to one that reflects upon and attempts to reframe its ethnographic legacies in the early twenty-first century, the museum has constructed a public in the Netherlands (and in Amsterdam in particular) as being made in the Dutch colonial world. In its exhibitionary strategy the museum has committed itself to a postcolonial task of "revisiting, remembering and . . . interrogating the colonial past," recollecting "the compelling seductions of colonial power."³⁶ Instead of embarking upon a recovery project that is either a corrective or an additive, it has utilized its own particular role within a history of colonialism, to challenge the bounded national state with its insular histories.

Museums and World History

The brief analysis of the two museums suggests that world historians can use their search for global associations to contextualize the emergence of museums, their collections and displays. This forms part of what Hall calls "the hidden history of production." It has also been suggested that analyzing the poetics of exhibiting "the practice of producing meaning through internal ordering and conjugation of the separate but related components of an exhibition"³⁷ enables historians to understand ways in which public pasts are represented—how the world is made and re-made in the museum. There are other areas of investigation that museums open up for world historians: international design histories, the circulation of cultural symbols (such as ancient Egypt and the dinosaur³⁸), and the development of academic disciplines and their relationship to the classifications and exhibitions in museums. By engaging with museums as sites of representation, and as institutions that produce history, notions of world history are extended not merely to include an additional area of research but also to discern how meanings of history are generated in the public domain. World history in and about the museum can open up debates about the representations of pasts, inviting us to consider the many ways that "pastness" is framed and claimed as history in its own right. And it invites us to ask: How and why it is that the personal collection of Farley and Germaine Berman has become a museum of world history in Anniston, Alabama?

Notes

1. This essay is based on research for the NRF funded Project on Public Pasts, based in the History Department at the University of the Western Cape. The financial support of the NRF towards this research is hereby acknowledged. Opinions expressed in this paper and conclusions arrived at are those of the author and are not necessarily to be attributed to the NRF. I would also like to thank my colleague Ciraj Rassool who has worked together with me on this research around the representation of history in museums.
2. Berman Museum of World History, www.bermanmuseum.org, accessed 13 August 2006. In its updated website the Berman museum maintains that "included in the collection are hundreds of bronzes, paintings by European and American artists, historically significant artifacts, ethnographic material, art from Asia, weaponry, and historical documents." The museum's two mottos are: "It's your world. Explore it!" and "Weaponry and Defenses that Changed Nations." www.bermanmuseum.org/aboutUs, accessed 2 September 2006.
3. Google search, "museums, world, history," www.google.com, 13 August 2006, 2 September 2006.
4. Stuart Hall, ed., *Representation: Cultural Representations and Signifying Practices*, (London: Sage, 1997), 160.
5. Tony Bennett, *The Birth of the Museum* (London and New York: Routledge, 1995), chapters 2 and 3.
6. Hall, *Representation*, 186.
7. Barbara Kirshenblatt-Gimblett, *Destination Culture* (Berkeley: University of California Press, 1998), 132.
8. Hall, *Representation*, 162.
9. See, for example, Patricia Davison, "Typecast: Representation of the Bushmen at the South African Museum," Public Archaeology 2 (2001): 3–20; and Pippa Skotnes, "The Politics of Bushman Representations," in Paul S. Landau and Deborah D. Kaspin, eds., Images and Empires: Visuality in Colonial and Postcolonial Africa (Berkeley: University of California Press, 2002), 253–274.
Phil Macnaghten and John Urry, Contested Natures (London: Sage, 1998), 15.
10. I am citing Premesh Lalu's forthcoming book, *In the Event of History: On the Postcolonial Critique of Apartheid* (forthcoming), introduction. Thanks to Premesh for allowing me to quote from his draft manuscript.
11. Bennett, *Birth of the Museum*, 153.
12. David Birmingham, *A Concise History of Portugal* (Cambridge: Cambridge University Press, 2003), 199; Christina Hippley, "Nowhere Man Who Packs Potent Punch," *Observer*, 26 July 1987.
13. E. H. Serra Brandão, "Message," in António Figueiredo, ed., *Bartolomeu Dias 1488–1988* (Lisbon: National Board for the Celebration of Portuguese Discoveries, 1988), 4–5.

14. Edward Cody, "There is a Feeling We Are Starting a New Cycle in Our History," *Washington Post*, 13 February 1988, p. G8; muweb.millersville.edu/~columbus/data/art/CODY-01.ART, accessed 29 May 2005.
15. Juliette Saunders, "Dias Festival is Aimed at all South Africans," *Evening Post*, 2 July 1987.
16. J. Clifford, *The Predicament of Culture: Twentieth Century Ethnography, Literature, and Art* (Cambridge, MA: Harvard University Press, 1988).
17. Hall, *Representation*, 161.
18. D. Van Duuren, "Introduction into the Colonial Collection," in KIT Tropenmuseum, "Dutch Colonialism: International Presentation of an Exhibition Concept" (Unpublished Workshop Report, Amsterdam, Tropenmuseum, 14–15 March 2001), 29.
19. J. Huub and H. van den Brink, *Tropen in Amsterdam: 70 jaar Koninklijk Instituut voor de Tropen* (Amsterdam: KIT, 1999), 78.
20. Van Duuren, "Introduction into the Colonial Collection," 29.
21. Ibid., 29-30; Huub and Van den Brink, *Tropen in Amsterdam*, 92–96.
22. Cited in S. Legêne, and E. Postel-Coster, "Isn't It All Culture: Culture and Dutch Development Policy in the Post-colonial Period," 277–279.
23. Legêne and Postel-Coster, "Isn't It All Culture," 281.
24. S. Legêne, "The Invisibility of the 'Colonial' Collection in the Tropenmuseum 1950–2000," in KIT Tropenmuseum, "Dutch Colonialism: International Presentation of an Exhibition concept," (unpublished workshop report, Amsterdam, Tropenmuseum, 14–15 March 2001), 31.
25. Legêne and Postel-Coster, "Isn't It All Culture," 281.
26. Clifford, *Predicament*, 222–227.
27. G. Staal and M. de Rijk, *IN side OUT ON site IN: Redesigning the National Museum of Ethnology Leiden The Netherlands* (Amsterdam: BIS, 2003), 144.
28. Gert Staal and Martin de Rijk, "Magische ontmoetingen: Magical encounters" (Leiden: Rijksmuseum voor Volkenkunde, 2003) (pamphlet).
29. Kirshenblatt-Gimblett, *Destination*, 136.
30. S. Legêne, "Raison d'être for Dutch Colonialism," in KIT Tropenmuseum, "Dutch Colonialism: International Presentation of an Exhibition Concept," 14–15 March 2001, 26.
31. Legêne, "Raison d'être for Dutch Colonialism," 28.
32. S. Legêne, "Multiculturalism and Colonial Culture," Opening speech at *Eastward Bound! Art, Culture, and Colonialism*, Tropenmuseum, Amsterdam, 29 January 2003.
33. Legêne, "Multiculturalism and Colonial Culture."
34. KIT Tropenmuseum, "Oostwaarts! Kuns, Kultuur en Kolonialisme. Een Dwarse Kijk op Koloniaal Verleden" (Amsterdam: KIT Tropenmuseum, 2003) (pamphlet).
35. Legêne, "Multiculturalism and Colonial Culture."
36. Leela Gandhi, *Postcolonial Theory: A Critical Introduction* (New York: Columbia University Press, 1998), 4.
37. Hall, *Representation*, 199, 168.
38. See W. J. T. Mitchell, *The Last Dinosaur Book* (Chicago: University of Chicago Press, 1998). Mitchell's claim to the status of the dinosaur as a totem of modernity relates to the ways it comes to symbolize social unity, acts as a figure of ancestry, and becomes an object of taboo and ritual. Its modernity derives from the dinosaur's emergence in the nineteenth century, the sense of modern time in which dinosaur narratives operate and the role of dinosaurs in forging a modern public citizenry (chapter 12).

CHAPTER 12

The World History Network—Facilitating Global Historical Research

Patrick Manning

The World History Network, established in its present form in 2004, has as its objective the facilitation of historical research at a global level. While many other institutions contribute to world-historical research, the Network is focused primarily on this task. The activities of the Network have been situated primarily in North America, its home base, but a substantial beginning has been made toward facilitating and publicizing world historical research in many areas of the world.

Current Network Activities

Entering the fourth year of its existence, the Network draws on modest amounts of funding from a variety of sources.[1] It sustains four major types of activity: a website, the convening of specialized conferences, print publications, and research projects. The website, first, is a comprehensive guide to online resources for research and teaching in world history. A database of over two hundred teaching and research resources, each categorized and introduced with a brief critical commentary, is shared by the teaching and research sides of the site. In addition the site provides access to major programs of graduate study, major journals in world history with tables of content, and announcements of conferences, prize competitions, and a selection of recent publications.

Secondly, the Network sponsors specialized research conferences, supplementing the conferences of major historical organizations. The 2006

Research Agenda Symposium focused on identifying research priorities in world history; a second conference on research agenda is planned for the 2008-2009 academic year. A third conference, providing a critical celebration of the life and work of Andre Gunder Frank, has been announced for April 2008. Each of these meetings, while held in the U.S., draws participants from all over the world.

Thirdly, the Network supports print publication. This volume is the second volume published through the efforts of the network; it was preceded by a volume highlighting the research of scholars trained in formal programs of world-historical study.[2] Future conferences are expected to result in publications of conference proceedings. Fourthly, the Network has begun to organize support for world historical research projects, as described later in this chapter.

In its governance, the Network is incorporated as a nonprofit corporation headed by a five-person Board of Directors, one of whom serves as president. An Advisory Board provides periodic commentary on the affairs of the Network, making recommendations especially on funding.[3] In 2006 the Network became an affiliate of the World History Association, and in the same year the members of its Board of Directors were appointed as members of the WHA Research Committee.[4] Thus the Network carries out its own activities, but reports on a number of its activities to the WHA.

A few other organizations parallel the World History Network, in that they support world-historical research in various ways. The Network seeks to maintain regular contact with them: they include the World History Association, the European Network in Universal and Global History (ENIUGH), the Research Institute of World History, World History For Us All, and the Golden Web project.[5]

Evolution of the World History Network

The Network emerged out a previous decade of building graduate study in world history. Only gradually did the need appear, out of that experience, for an independent institution, world-wide in its scope, and focused primarily on facilitating research in world history. The experiences that led to formation of the World History Network were those of the doctoral program in world history at Northeastern University (beginning in 1994), the World History Center at Northeastern University (1994–2004), and the project for creation of the World History Network website (2001–2004).

The doctoral program at Northeastern University, focusing almost entirely on world history, admitted an average of three students per year from 1994 to 2000, and declined somewhat thereafter. University approval of the program in 1993 included the stipulation that future hires would expand the faculty in world history, but in practice no more than two specialists in world history were ever employed in the department. With so many competing demands in the university and in the History Department, few resources in faculty appointments or staff support were allocated to world history. Further, external fellowship support for students was scarce, as world-history proposals tended to lose out in competition with area-studies dissertation work. Nevertheless, a curriculum for research specialization in world history was developed and successfully implemented for a time. By 2004, ten world history PhDs had been awarded, and in virtually every case the degree recipients had found employment as professors of world history.[6]

The World History Center at Northeastern, created along with the history PhD program, was to be a research center somewhat parallel to area-studies centers. It facilitated research of doctoral students at Northeastern and nearby institutions, for instance through conduct of a World History Seminar, in which local and visiting scholars gave nearly a hundred presentations over the course of a decade.[7] As with the doctoral program, the university hoped that external funding would provide support for the center. External support came in the form of project grants, but the center never had support for dedicated staff. It obtained some small research grants, but most of its $2 million in external funding came from projects to support teaching: multimedia instruction materials, supplementary materials for textbooks, and professional development workshops for teachers. This work on teaching did provide support and experience for the doctoral students who carried out much of the work. From 1998 to 2002 the World History Resource Center—a teacher resource library and center for teacher workshops—developed a separate identity from the World History Center, and conducted numerous regional and national teacher workshops.

Nevertheless, the shortage of resources in the university, and the reluctance of funding agencies to support research in world history, led to the conclusion that the Center was unsustainable in its current form. As founder and director of the center, I decided in 2002 that the center would close, and that decision was implemented in the spring of 2004. A wrap-up conference was held in March of 2004, and the center closed in June.[8]

Yet the center completed one last major project before closing. When the National Endowment for the Humanities opened a competition in 2000 for a comprehensive world history website, emphasizing both teaching and research, the World History Center applied and won the award. From 2001 to 2004 construction of the website took place, with an emphasis on creating a critical guide to resources, rather than a definitive summary of world history. The website was organized with overlapping teaching and research sections: it centered on a database that could link to thousands of sites, each of them described in systematic terms. Co-director Heidi Roupp, having just completed a term as WHA president, led in building the teaching side of the website. Under her leadership, a preliminary WHN website provided current teaching materials for users from 2002 to 2004. Additional aspects of the website included descriptions of major programs of graduate study, lists of world-historical journals and their tables of contents, and space for discussion of current research. The website was released to the public in July 2004, and remains active. For its initial two years, the website had to be maintained primarily through volunteer labor, but thereafter it began to gain a systematic staff. It took major funding, such as that from NEH, to create this website; it was to require additional major support to sustain it.

In sum, the experience of ten years' work at Northeastern showed that, while an energetic local group could prepare PhD graduates with strong research skills in world history, virtually all of whom would gain employment within their field in higher education, the resources of a single university could not sustain the program. Collaboration among the small existing groups seemed the only possible way to enable a conception of world history specialization to grow. An independent organization, not tied to a single university, presented the most logical option for facilitating ties among researchers. For the organization to base its activities on a website would help with communication among the far-flung participants. Thus it was decided to form the World History Network, Inc., which would become proprietor of the World History Network website. The new organization maintained the archives of the World History Center, but otherwise ended the Center's affiliation with Northeastern University.[9] With these steps, the World History Network launched itself as an independent, nonprofit corporation, and began to elaborate a more wide-ranging focus on research in world history.

Research in World History

Research in world history takes place in a variety of institutional and organizational frameworks, and is conducted by scholars with varying backgrounds and varying academic identities. Such research is usually conducted by individuals, though occasionally it is collaborative or even supported by major research grants. To categorize the background of researchers, one may distinguish individual research by self-trained scholars (mostly at senior levels), research by scholars who have had some training in world history (for instance, as a minor field in doctoral studies), and research by scholars who have completed comprehensive and specialized programs in world history. World historians are subdivided in their identities in other ways as well. Various labels have developed to differentiate various communities of "worldish" historians with specializations in big history, global history, transnational history, international history, not to mention such nearby communities as those of Atlantic history, area-studies history, and imperial history.[10]

For all the richness of these varying approaches to history on a large scale, the field remains limited seriously by its reliance on self-trained scholars. The shortage of formal, graduate-level training in world-historical analysis is arguably the greatest limitation on the expanded strength and scope of research. Graduate programs do exist at a few universities in North America, Europe, Australia, and East Asia, but progress in the expansion of these programs and their production of PhDs is very slow. The World History Network is not well placed to contribute much to establishing new programs of graduate study in world history.

But the Network can contribute to the productivity of existing programs by facilitating contacts among them, ensuring exchange of information and curricular ideas, research materials, and even actual faculty members and students. Simply listing and describing the programs on the Network website is a start; encouraging contacts at international conferences is another useful tactic.

In addition the Network can pursue a campaign, first proposed some years ago, to create post-doctoral appointments as an effective way to expand the number of specialized world historians. That is, if funds were available to support a postdoctoral fellowship, based in an existing graduate program in world history, awards could be made to recent PhD-holders who have some background in world history, but who could substantially strengthen their expertise in a year or two of teaching and research in collaboration with leading scholars in the field. This idea first developed at a World History Association meeting in 2003, but funds have yet to be located to implement it. In a second dimension of building skills of researchers, the Network can hope to facilitate location of support for researchers to work in archives well supplied with world historical data, such as the national archives in Lisbon, Amsterdam, London, Beijing, and Washington, and the archives of international organizations in Geneva and New York.

The Network has already achieved advances in another area: debating the research agenda of world history. In late 2005 the Network decided to sponsor an international conference to debate the research priorities of world history; in early 2006 the World History Association became a co-sponsor. The conference itself was held in Boston in November of 2006: its results comprise the opening chapter of this volume.

Further, the Network can participate in the creation of world-historical databases. The combination of national governments, international organizations, and university research groups have developed fairly comprehensive, global databases addressing the last half of the twentieth century. For earlier times, however, the data remain scattered and disaggregated, except for data on such extraordinary nations as Sweden. One response to the need for data has been the development of historical databases on various specific topics, especially within economic history. Yet another dimension is the attempt to develop systematic, worldwide data for periods before the mid-twentieth century. The World History Network is now associated with two small projects to begin the work of designing comprehensive historical databases and assembling empirical databases to make them comprehensive.[11]

Global Studies Approaches

World history, though a cosmopolitan field of study, can only go so far within its disciplinary boundaries. The projects and activities described above, while promising substantial advances through linking up otherwise isolated historians, do not do much to link historians to the advances in neighboring disciplines. One may ask, then, whether there is something to be gained by connecting world historians to the developing programs of "global studies." Global studies centers and programs have proliferated in major universities, especially in the United States but in virtually every region of the world as well. These programs, however, have focused rather specifically on contemporary politics, economics, and occasionally environmental concerns, rather than on the full range of global problems deserving of analysis.[12] The enterprise of global studies, as practiced so far, has included very little in the way of history, and little in the humanities.

Another approach to global studies would be to create centers for global studies more fully parallel to those of area studies. Area Studies scholarship, developed from the mid-twentieth century, has been multidisciplinary, with regional interplay of social sciences and humanities. Area studies scholarship has relied heavily on history, which has been important in anchoring the identity of each regional program of study—no less for Africa and Latin America than for East Asia, South Asia, and Russian and East European Studies.

A still more comprehensive approach to global studies might prove to be productive for the development of world history, and more productive in general as a field of knowledge. It could include history and the humanities, it could address long time frames as well as the immediate present and future, it could encompass varying spatial frameworks from the local to the global, and it could become a realm of encounter of various theoretical approaches.

The World History Network is beginning experiments with the latter two approaches to global studies. These experiments have begun locally at the University of Pittsburgh, but it is anticipated that they will expand to collaboration with other global studies centers and programs. Possible benefits of this comprehensive approach to global studies could emerge in at least four general areas. First, this approach would put the field of world history into institutional contact with other fields in social sciences, in humanities, and in natural sciences. Second, it would enable world history to work systematically with area-studies scholars (who tend to work at regional, continental, or civilizational levels), and would facilitate geographic analysis at varying spatial scope. Third, a broad approach to global studies should bring additional breadth to the temporal framework. The field of history has mostly focused on modern and early modern periods—for instance, emphasizing the histories of nations, which have existed for roughly two centuries. Empires, however, however, have existed for five millennia, and environmental processes evolve over both short-term and very long-term paces. All of these factors are worthy of world-historical analysis. Finally, the broad approach to global studies should result in the linkage of theories that have been developed in specific arenas. Historians may have a special role to play in nurturing the links among various theories, notably in the interplay of political, social, and demographic factors. At present, the various fields of environmental studies have shown leadership in transdisciplinary work. While it is unlikely that an advanced form of global studies would bring simultaneous advance in all of these areas, the point of listing these suggestions is that a more comprehensive approach may facilitate connections in research revealing new patterns in historical change at the global level.

Toward a Global Discourse on the Global Past

The field of history, more than most arenas of scholarship, centers its study at the national level. Its institutions of study, its academic journals, are organized primarily at the national level, or in aggregations of closely related nations. Not only are the historical interpretations focused primarily at the national level, but the authors of historical works work limit most of their intellectual exchange to discussions with others of the same national unit. In a world that we widely and readily label as globalizing, it is time to give adequate emphasis to the global side of history. This ought to be done along at least two axes: the development of interpretations of global patterns in the past, and the creation of a global historical discourse. The earlier parts of this chapter have focused primarily on the conduct of research yielding large-scale interpretations of the past. These final paragraphs give more attention to creating a global discourse.

Of the various past efforts to create global discourse on history, the one that stands out most was led by UNESCO in its early days, in the 1940s and 1950s: UNESCO took under its wing the Comité International des Sciences

Historiques (CISH), and supported creation of a new historical journal and a general history of the world.[13] In fact that effort was focused more on creating a world-wide discourse than on developing global interpretations. The effort created a number of volumes, but did not succeed in creating an ongoing, transnational community of historical scholars. Indeed, UNESCO in its early days also launched a world-wide investigation of the history of science, and an initial volume of the *History of Mankind: Scientific and Cultural Development* appeared in 1963. This divergence in the efforts of historians and historians of science began to be reconsidered only later, after both initial UNESCO projects had been abandoned.[14]

We now are in the midst of another effort to create a global discourse on history, as world-historical research and analysis is developing in numerous regions and numerous disciplines. Given today's interplay of world-historical research with studies in social sciences, natural sciences, and humanities, it is difficult to believe that the divergence of the early UNESCO projects will be repeated. There is every reason for world historians to be connected organizationally and intellectually to each other, to scholars in other fields of history, and to colleagues in other disciplines worldwide. Nevertheless, the development of such connections is proceeding at a slow pace, and world historians' practice of working as self-supporting individual scholars is not well designed to speed up these connections. The grass-roots strength of world historians, developing new and global insights from many vantage points, needs to be complemented by a stronger network of historians and more formalized links to other groups of scholars. It will require a proactive approach for world historians to gain the organizational breadth and strength necessary to establish good communication with the sociologists, art historians, and environmental scientists who are also working to assemble large-scale interpretations of the past.

One such step is in process: the creation of an International Network of World History Organizations (INWHO), which can become an affiliate of CISH and put world historians formally on the program at the quinquennial CISH conferences. Thanks in particular to the energies of Matthias Middell (Leipzig University) and David Christian (San Diego State University), the World History Association and the European Network in Universal and Global History are cooperating to form the new network and to request affiliation with CISH. This structure will have the advantage of maintaining and strengthening existing organizations, but also providing a space for development of participating groups of world historians based in Asia, Africa, and Latin America. It can strengthen the worldwide dialogue among world historians. Most importantly, it may be a step at the global level toward the formal recognition of world history, in all its forms, as an established arena of scientific study, worthy of support for its research and valuable as a field of study with which scholars in other fields should conduct exchanges.

Notes

1. These have included royalties from sales of *Migration in Modern World History, 1500–2000* (Wadsworth Publishing, 2000), produced by the World History Center; conference support from the School of Arts & Sciences at the University of Pittsburgh; and conference support from publishers.
2. Patrick Manning, ed., *World History: Global and Local Interactions* (Princeton, NJ: Markus Wiener Publications, 2005).
3. Officers are Patrick Manning, President; H. Parker James, Treasurer; and other board members are Deborah Smith Johnston, David Kalivas, and Stephen H. Rapp. Advisory Board members are Stanley Katz (Princeton University), Janice Reiff (UCLA), Heidi Roupp (Aspen, CO), James Stellar (Northeastern University), and Heather Streets (Washington State University). The Network is incorporated in the state of Massachusetts. For further details see www.worldhistorynetwork.org/dev, "About Us."
4. The Research Committee of the World History Association included as its members in 2006 and 2007 Patrick Manning, chair, Zvi Ben-Dor Benite, H. Parker James, Deborah Smith Johnston, David Kalivas, Adam McKeown, and Stephen H. Rapp.
5. World History Association (www.thewha.org), the European Network in Universal and Global History—ENIUGH (www.uni-leipzig.de/~eniugh/index.php), the Research Institute for World History (www.history.l.chiba-u.jp/~riwh/index.html), World History For Us All (worldhistoryforusall.sdsu.edu/), and The Golden Web Foundation (www.goldenweb.org/).
6. For the eight PhD dissertations completed by the end of 2003, see www.worldhistorycenter.org, "Graduate Study." The same page describes the dissertation of eight further students in this group who completed their degrees in 2004 (5), 2006 (1), and 2007 (2).
7. www.worldhistorycenter.org, "Seminar."
8. For the conference website, see 134.241.47.94/NextTenYears/index.html; proceedings of the conference were published as Manning, ed., *World History*.
9. In its first three years the Network retained its base in Boston, though some activities moved to Pittsburgh as the president took up employment at the University of Pittsburgh.
10. For a recent discussion of the various labels adopted by historians working at scales beyond the national, see "*AHR* Conversation: On Transnational History," *American Historical Review* 111 (2006): 1441–1464.

11. The projects are "World-Historical Database Design Group" and "Global Studies over Time: An Online Database Collection," each supported by funding from the University of Pittsburgh.
12. In secondary schools in the U.S., in contrast, "global studies" generally refers to curricula centered on geography and comparative cultures.
13. CISH was founded in Geneva in 1926; the postwar journal was *Cahers d'Histoire Mondiale* or *Journal of World History*. CISH is usually known by its French-language acronym rather than, in English, the International Committee of Historical Sciences. On the project of a general history, see Gilbert Allardyce, "Toward World History: American Historians and the Coming of the World History Course," *Journal of World History* 1 (1990): 23–76.
14. Libby Robin and Will Steffen, "World History without Historians? Science in Search of Sustainability" (unpublished paper). I am grateful to the authors for permission to cite this study. The organizations for history and history of science were affiliated with quite different sections of UNESCO: CISH (history) affiliated with the International Council of Philosophy and Human Sciences, while the International Union for the History of Science affiliated with the International Council of Scientific Unions.

Notes on Contributors

Ahmed Ibrahim Abushouk
Professor, Department of History, International Islamic University Malaysia, Kuala Lumpur, Malaysia.

Shigeru Akita
Professor, Department of World History, Osaka University, Osaka, Japan.

Gareth Austin
Senior Lecturer, Department of Economic History, London School of Economics, London, United Kingdom.

Jerry H. Bentley
Professor, Department of History, University of Hawai'i; editor, Journal of World History, Honolulu, United States.

David Christian
Professor, Department of History, San Diego State University, San Diego, United States.

Marilyn Lake
Professor, Department of Politics, La Trobe University, Melbourne, Australia.

Patrick Manning
Andrew W. Mellon Professor of World History, Department of History, University of Pittsburgh Pittsburgh, United States; President, World History Network, Inc.

Matthias Middell
Professor, Department of History, Leipzig University, Leipzig, Germany.

Shingo Minamizuka
Professor, Department of International Communications, Hosei University, Tokyo, Japan; Director, Research Institute of World History.

Katja Naumann
PhD candidate, Department of History, Leipzig University, Leipzig, Germany.

Diego Olstein
Lecturer in History, Hebrew University of Jerusalem, Jerusalem, Israel.

Heather Streets
Associate Professor, Department of History, Washington State University, Pullman, United States.

Swarnalatha Potukuchi
IGCSE and IB Teacher in History at the Dhirubhai Ambani International School, Mumbai, India.

Leslie Witz
Senior Lecturer, Department of History, University of the Western Cape, Cape Town, South Africa.

www.ingramcontent.com/pod-product-compliance
Lightning Source LLC
Chambersburg PA
CBHW020948230426
43666CB00005B/227